WHAT LOVE REQUIRES

Following God's Path to Deeper Relationships

ELLE PAGE

Bible Verses

The translation used will be in parentheses after the Bible reference.

NIV–New International Version, Zondervan

MSG–The Message, Eugene H. Peterson, 2005, NavPress

AMP–Amplified Bible, Lockman Foundation, 2001, Zondervan

TPT–The Passion Translation, Brian Simmons, 2020, BroadStreet Publishing Group LLC

Verses in bold are my emphases

ISBN 978-1-7370903-0-4

www.Elle-Page.com

DEDICATION

To my Lord, Jesus Christ, who put
these words in my heart and mind.

To my husband, David, who believed in
me first and advocated for this book.

To my friend and mentor, Ruth Craig, who
introduced me to plugging into
my Ultimate Power Source.

TABLE OF CONTENTS

INTRODUCTION

On my professional journey, I have been blessed to work with thousands of men and women in their quest to be their best. As I have trained and coached them—in the private sector, government, higher education, and the church—they discovered that the principles they learned also served them at home and in their communities.

Let me introduce you to a few of them. Maybe you can relate to their challenges. As I have in the other stories I will share, I've changed client names to ensure their privacy.

Arturo was a star in his company because of his extraordinary technical skills, but the way he treated his employees was diminishing his effectiveness.

Irina cherished her husband's family, but she didn't know how to communicate lovingly when they unintentionally offended her or broke her boundaries.

Eliana's team was operating out of competition, not teamwork. Unhealthy conflict was widespread, and trust was at an all-time low.

Newly married Destiny and Farrell learned that living together came with a wide variety of new conflicts. Did those disagreements mean that love was fading?

Victor felt unfulfilled and despondent at work, but wasn't sure why. He didn't want to seek a new job without understanding the source of his discontent.

Joshua was a wizard of an engineer, but his employees complained that he never listened to them.

London's husband had left her for her best friend. London was left feeling betrayed, lonely, angry and bitter.

Noelle was a savvy, fast-talking executive who did not know what empathy was—or when her employees needed it.

The tools I will introduce to you helped each of these individuals take a giant leap forward in their quest to be their best and reflect the love of God. I pray that you, too, will add a skill or two to your relationship tool belt so that through you, the world will see and hear Jesus more often.

The book is organized so that each chapter builds on the one before it. But, if you'd like to go straight to a solution you need, or the topic that most resonates with you, look at the Table of Contents or the last chapter, Tying it All Together, which lists the key lessons from each chapter. Appendix A also offers various ways to approach the information. Let's start the journey!

> *Now may the God who brought us peace… work perfection into every part of you giving you all that you need to fulfill your destiny. And may he express through you all that is excellent and pleasing to him through your life-union with Jesus the Anointed One who is to receive all glory forever! Amen!* (Hebrews 13:20-21 TPT)

CHAPTER ONE

THE QUEST

I had been praying for three years. Three long years. *God, how can I be significant for you in my next season of life?* Asking. Listening. Seeking. Waiting. I longed for a door to be opened. I was on a quest and determined not to give up.

During those three years of expectant prayer, I was methodically reducing my full-time leadership training and consulting work, and my travel schedule was ramping down from three weeks each month to one. I was absolutely confident that God would answer my ongoing prayer, show me his plan, and give me renewed purpose, but I confess I was getting impatient with his timing. The planner in me wanted his answer to come *now*, and my practical side expected that God would send me off to an organization that confronted human trafficking or abortion—two issues about which I had long been passionate. I investigated several relevant non-profits, but none of them seemed to be the right fit, and I neither felt nor heard a specific calling. *It will be just like God,* I thought, *to reveal His plan to me at the last minute.*

Then on March 1, 2019 in the middle of the night, when God often gets my attention, I was overwhelmed with ideas. I got up, threw on a robe, and grabbed my computer. Concepts poured out of my heart and soul as easily as water over a cliff. The Holy Spirit reminded me of a profound quote from nationally known pastor and author, Andy Stanley, that was driving my writing. "In every dealing with someone**, before every statement or response to anyone,** a follower of Jesus should first ask themselves: What does love require of me?"[i]

I am very pragmatic, and I value simplicity, so when I originally heard Stanley's question it struck a resonant chord in me. I found I liked it better than the well-known challenge from years ago, "What Would Jesus Do?" Stanley's question spoke to personal responsibility, one of my core values. When we ask, "What does love require of me?" it takes us right to *our* choices and *our* actions rather than thinking of Jesus' likely actions *as the Son of God*—who can do what I cannot!

Stanley's challenge also made me think of Viktor Frankl (1905-1997), an Austrian Holocaust survivor, neurologist, psychiatrist and author. In my consulting practice, I often use a concept that is believed to have been articulated by him. "Between stimulus and response, there is space. In that space is our power to choose our response. In our response lies our growth and our freedom."

The pieces were falling into place for me. **In every moment we are to choose love**. God had answered my prayer. I was being called to teach the Body of Christ about the choice points we have in each moment and the interpersonal skills and tools we need to respond in love. God prepared me well. I had been teaching people in the secular world for over two decades about how to communicate with respect and kindness, how to build trust, and to appreciate the people with whom they worked. Adding the Word of God to my teaching repertoire seemed the most natural thing to do. I loved the thought of turning Jesus' command to love one another into practical application. God had set a quest in my heart.

Before 6:30 that morning, I had completed a full outline of a 20-hour class. His timing was perfect and gave me five months to write the curriculum before I completed the switch to part-time consulting work. I used every bit of that time preparing for the class I started that fall, calling it, *What Does Love Require?* My prayer for ten women to sign-up, was answered by God with an abundant fifty students!

Our Quest

What is God's quest for *us*? Conveniently, a wise scribe asked Jesus this question. Mark shares this exchange with us in his Gospel.

> *Then one of the scribes came up and listened to them arguing [with one another], and noticing that Jesus answered them well, asked Him,* ***"Which commandment is first and most important of all?"***
>
> *Jesus answered, "The first and most important one is: 'Hear, O Israel the Lord our God is one Lord, and you shall love the Lord your God with all your heart, and with all your soul (life), and with all your mind (thought, understanding), and with all your strength.' This is the second: 'You shall [unselfishly] love your neighbor as yourself.' There is no other commandment greater than these."* (Mark 12:28-31 AMP)

Love is undeniably God's top priority. How does God tell us to go about demonstrating that love? A chief way is by loving his people. By "his people" he doesn't mean people who believe what you believe, or who go to your church, or people who love you first. He means **all the people he created**. EVERYONE.

When Jesus was teaching about loving one's neighbor, an attorney asked Jesus how he would define "neighbor". Jesus responded with the parable of the Good Samaritan (Luke 10:25-37). Let me paraphrase it with a modern twist. As a man walked down a city street late one night, someone knocked him down, brutally beat him, robbed him and left him for dead. Early the next morning, a pastor came upon him and, not really wanting to get involved, walked to the other side of the street. A priest walked by next and, fearing for his own life, quickly stepped around him. After a time, a terrorist on the FBI's most-wanted list came by. He had compassion on the beaten man, took a first-aid kit out of his backpack, bandaged his wounds and went back for his car. He laid the bruised man in the back seat, took him to the local hospital, pre-paid for his care, and promised to cover any additional costs.

> Jesus then asked, "*Which of these proved to be a neighbor to the abused man?" The attorney answered, "The one who showed compassion and mercy to him." Jesus responded, "**Go and constantly do the same.**"* (Luke 10:37 AMP)

And that, my friends, is God's quest for us. Go! Constantly see people—really see them—and intentionally love them even at a cost to yourself. And then do it again and again. Jesus' primary message was clear: **everyone should actively love everyone else all the time.** He was also issuing a caution. Jesus was pointing out that even the most religious people may choose *not* to love, and the most unlikely people choose love.

The Apostle Paul gives us more specifics on what love requires.

> *Therefore, as God's chosen people, holy and dearly loved,* **clothe yourselves with compassion, kindness, humility, gentleness and patience. Bear with each other and forgive one another** *if any of you have a grievance against someone. Forgive* **as the Lord forgave you.** *And over all these virtues put on love, which binds them all together in perfect unity.* (Colossians 3:10 NIV)

What do compassion, kindness, humility, gentleness and patience *look like*? *Sound* like? How do we "clothe" ourselves in them? Must we bear with all difficult people? Aren't some things unforgivable? There's more.

> *Let the peace of Christ rule in your hearts, since as members of one body you were called to peace. And be thankful. Let the message of Christ dwell among you richly as you teach and admonish one another with all wisdom through psalms, hymns, and songs from the Spirit, singing to God with gratitude in your hearts.* (Colossians 3:15-16 NIV)

How can we live in peace with all the conflict the world imposes? I can't even live in peace in my home! And with all the social unrest these days, I often feel more fearful or skeptical than thankful.

But there's more.

> *Offer your bodies as a living sacrifice, holy and pleasing to God, this is your true and proper worship. Do not conform to the pattern of this world, but be transformed by the renewing of your mind… Be devoted* **to one another in love. Honor one another above yourselves.** (Rom 12:1-2, 10 NIV)

It's hard enough to be devoted to my spouse, my parents, and my children. Who has time to be devoted to *everyone*? Are we to honor others above ourselves? How does that look in the actual world of work, competition, social media and polarized politics?

And, yes, there's still more!

> *You, my brothers and sisters, were called to be free. But do not use your freedom to indulge the flesh; rather,* ***serve one another humbly in love****. For the entire law is fulfilled in keeping this one command: "Love your neighbor as yourself."* (Galatians 5:13-14 NIV)

The love God requires sounds utterly impossible. Serve others? Humbly? With love? All at the same time?!

Love in Action

The books of James and 1 John drive home the ultimate point.

> *Do not merely listen to the word, and so deceive yourselves.* ***Do what it says.*** (James 1:22 NIV)

> *Dear children, let us not love with words or speech but with* ***actions and in truth****.* (1 John 3:18 NIV)

And the Amplified Bible translation definitely amps it up!

> *But* ***prove yourselves doers of the word*** *[****actively and continually obeying*** *God's precepts], and not merely listeners [who hear the word but fail to internalize its meaning], deluding yourselves [by unsound reasoning contrary*

to the truth]. (James 1:22 AMP)

Knowing is not enough, we must apply. Willing is not enough, we must do. *Johann Wolfgang Von Goethe*

We are called to obey God by doing what His Word says, to be a compassionate, kind, humble, gentle, patient, forgiving, peaceful, thankful person who not only puts up with people but actually honors them, is loyal to them, and is willing to serve them with humility. And doing *all of this all the time to all people* is love—lavish love. This is one TALL order!

An Easy-ish Formula—Respond-ability

Stanley and Frankl[ii] hold an excellent key for how to choose love in any moment. Both advocate the simple practice of **taking a pause before responding**. What a concept! Unlike animals that react by instinct, we have the gift of free will, of *choice*. We can stop, seek the advice of the Holy Spirit—our moment-by-moment, ever available, life-transforming Helper—and *then* respond; we have the incredible power of choice. In a 2020 sermon, Stanley called "Respond-ability" our Secret Superpower. In any moment, before responding, I can skip the God-given pause and do what my *instincts* tell me—defensive behaviors built up over years to protect me from perceived harm. OR I can choose to consult the Holy Spirit and ***do what the Word says.*** I love how Sarah Young paraphrases Psalm 105:4 in her *Jesus Calling* devotional, "A renewed mind is Presence-focused. Train your mind to seek Me in every moment, every situation."[iii]

Not for Our Salvation

Friend, hear me loud and clear. This is not salvation by works. By taking on these practices, God will not love us more. We are already his beloved children. This is not performance-based salvation. The blood of Christ saves us, period. Yet, after the price for our sins had already been paid, look what Jesus said to his disciples after his resurrection.

> *All authority in heaven and on earth has been given to me.* **Therefore, go** *and make disciples of all nations, baptizing them in the name of the Father and of the Son, and of the Holy Spirit, and* **teaching them to obey everything I have commanded you.** *And surely, I am with you always,* [in the form of the Holy Spirit] *to the very end of the age.* (Matthew 28:18-20 NIV)

We are saved by his work, **but he left us with work to do.** We often focus on the "go and make disciples" and neglect the part about teaching and obeying all that Jesus commanded. But Jesus emphasized each of these tasks. Remember, obeying means *serving everyone, humbly, with love* (Gal 5:13-14 NIV)

The familiar love chapter in the Bible, read at many weddings, sets the bar for love even higher:

> *Love is patient and kind; love does not envy or boast; it is not arrogant or rude. It does not insist on its own way; it is not irritable or resentful; it does not rejoice at wrongdoing, but rejoices with the truth. Love bears all things, believes all things, hopes all things, endures all things.* (I Corinthians 13:4-7, ESV)

Over forty years ago, I stood at the altar, gazing into my fiancé's eyes, and earnestly professed these commitments. A week later, I felt like a liar, a failure or (sometimes) justified in not following through! Relationships are hard even when we are madly in love. Loving others—loving our enemies—as Jesus commands is a lifelong journey. I hope I will give you a fresh jolt of enthusiasm for that trip.

Imagine what it would be like for people to see the gospel through the *Christ-like actions they experience in you.* I will introduce you to—or remind you of—communication skills that will enable you to do what love requires, what our God who *is love* requires. You will grow to more consistently reflect Christ's love, experience the joy and blessing that brings, and draw others to Christ in a natural, magnetic way.

> Realizing that you have the power to choose and making the most of your choice is where the work of being an effective person takes place.
>
> *Stephen R. Covey*

Self-reflection

1. How do you show love daily? What are some acts of love you intentionally choose to do or easily do as a natural part of your personality?

2. What makes *you* feel loved and valued? What do people do for you that makes you experience love?

3. In what situations do you struggle to love others? Yourself?

CHAPTER TWO

LISTENING WITH HEART

> *My dear brothers and sisters, take note of this: Everyone should be* **quick to listen**, *slow to speak and slow to become angry, because human anger does not produce the righteousness that God desires.* (James 1:19-20 NIV)

When we communicate with someone, we can choose to listen, ask questions or speak. We will explore each of these three modes of communication in the next three chapters, but we'll start with the one James encourages us to do quickly. It's also the communication mode most appreciated. When I ask people what makes them feel loved, a vast majority say it is having someone really listen to them. Listening well to another human being is one of the most loving gifts you can give—and you can give it easily and often.

I can hear your objections already!

- "It takes so much time!"
- "I get so distracted—or bored."
- "If I listen well to [I know you are thinking of a specific name], they'll never stop talking!"

I will address these objections. I promise. For now, try to put them aside as we unpack this under-used demonstration of love that God's Word says we should be quick to use.

Currently on Amazon, there are over 600 books on listening—which tells me this is something that doesn't come as naturally to us as James implies. Why is listening so hard when it seems so passive? I don't have to *do* anything to have your sound waves hit my ears.

Here's the challenge: while people talk at about 125 words per minute, your God-designed brain can process at between 400-500 words per minute.[iv] You were created with excess brain capacity! (I know it doesn't always feel that way, but research proves it is true.) While your friend or co-worker is telling you about the challenges of his/her day, you can nod your head while simultaneously thinking about the emails you need to answer, what you are going to do tomorrow or endless other things that are not at all connected to what your friend is saying. Listening with love is all about how you use your excess brain capacity and how selfless that choice is.

There are four ways to use that excess capacity while you are listening. I won't sugarcoat it. They're listed from most selfish to most self*less*. As you read through the descriptions, consider what your primary listening style might be.

1. Not Really Listening
2. Self-focused Listening
3. Other-focused Listening
4. Hyper-focused Listening

1. Not Really Listening—I'm Checked Out

One way to use your excess brain capacity when someone is talking is to think about *anything else.* You go on a journey of thought so that while you are physically there (in person, on the computer screen for a virtual meeting or on the phone) you aren't really present; your mind is miles away. Most of us can spot the body language indicating this mode of listening pretty quickly—the lack of eye contact or glazed eyes, the body turned slightly away, or the dead give-away, an irrelevant comment or question.

Here's how Not Really Listening sounds:

My husband: I had an awful day at work.
Me: I forgot to get something out of the freezer for dinner!
My husband: They split my commission for last month's sales with Bob!
Me: I guess we're going to have to go out tonight.

No one will experience love with this kind of "listening."

2. Self-focused Listening—Me, Me, Me

Another way to choose to use that excess brain capacity is to think about how what you are hearing relates to you, which, consciously or subconsciously, suddenly makes the conversation **all about you**. You hear the speaker's topic, but instead of listening, you go right to the "tape" in your brain, press "play" and review all the information you know about that topic. As in "Not Really Listening", you are physically present in the conversation on the other end of the phone, but your mind is not. Instead, you are busy comparing what you are hearing to something similar you did in the past or applying it to something you want to do in the future. You are not present. And at the first pause, you put the focus on you.

Here's how self-focused listening sounds:

Speaker: We just took an incredible trip to Europe.

Me: I love Europe! We've been six times! Our first trip was on a cruise to the Mediterranean, so we could visit seven countries in ten days. It really helped us determine where we wanted to travel next.

Speaker: We started out in Germany.

Me: Oh! Our second trip to Europe was to Italy. The food was amazing, and the scenery was incredible! I've been to Germany, but we didn't get there until our third or fourth trip. [and on I go. Just like that, I have hijacked the conversation and moved the focus from my friend to me.]

Sound familiar? When this was first described to me in my coach certification training, it hit me hard. I had been doing this most of my life with the purpose of *building connection*! I didn't intend to be rude or unloving! My *intent* in sharing my stories was to let people know I understood exactly what they were saying, to highlight what we had in common. I wanted to enhance my relationships.

In the illustration above, did I learn *anything* about her trip to Europe? No. I was too busy using my excess brain capacity to relive *my* trip. My friend lost her train of thought and, as I think back on the look on her face, I didn't get the sense she felt valued, loved or understood. I shut her down. I diminished the relationship.

Bottom-line: when I choose self-focused listening, I interrupt the speaker to bring the spotlight on me. And even if I don't say all those things out loud, I've taken a **journey of thought in my mind** and have missed all that she was saying.

I believe that this is the default mode of listening for most of us; we do not consciously *choose* it, we just fall into it. We are self-focused, sinful humans. If we fail to take that pause to ask, "What does love require?" we are likely going to fall into self-focused listening and either share our own story or go on a silent trip in our minds.

There are a few times self-focused listening is appropriate. When you are listening to your doctor, or an advisor, you *should* be thinking about what they are recommending. Has it worked for you in the past? Might it work in the future? But the vast majority of times, when we want to shine Christ's light, we will use other-focused listening.

3. Other-focused Listening—I Choose You

A third way to listen is to make it all about the speaker. Less of me, more of them. To listen well in this mode, we humans have to consciously *choose* to tamp down our own thoughts which I refer to as the "tapes" or "noise" in my head, and instead use our excess brain capacity to be fully present and interested in the speaker. We have to tap into our Respond-ability Superpower. Our motive for listening shifts from wanting to share our own story, even in an effort to connect, to being very curious about *the speaker's unique perspective*—even on a topic you may already know a lot about.

Here's how it sounds.

Speaker: We just took an incredible trip to Europe.

Me: Wonderful! Tell me about it.

Speaker: We started out in Germany, landing in Berlin and traveling south from there.

Me: [*I've been there three times. Yipes! It's not about me. What does love require? I need to find out the speaker's perspective on Germany.*]

What did you find incredible about Germany? [*I've let the*

speaker know I was listening by repeating the word she used in her opening.]

Speaker: We loved the people and the food. Our visit to Dachau, the former concentration camp, especially moved me. [*and she's off, sharing something and I am learning something—not just about Germany but more importantly about her]*

Me: [*I am listening so well! She has such a different take on Germany. I thought it was all beer halls, red cabbage and bratwursts. Boy, that was fun… Oops! I've got to get back to focusing on her.*]

I'm sorry, I missed your last point. I want to be sure I see Dachau through your eyes. You walked through the prisoners' barracks and felt….

Speaker: [*Shares interesting details, emotions and paints a vivid picture of her trip*]

Have you ever been to Germany? What did you find incredible?

[*Now she's genuinely passing the topic to me. She's felt heard, valued and understood and wants to hear my perspective. We've connected!*]

Do you understand how this is serving with humility and, "*not thinking of yourself more highly than you ought*"? That's what we show when we choose other-focused listening. But our minds are active, and we have thoughts about the topics a speaker mentions. It is **a moment-by-moment choice** to keep the focus on the speaker, to learn, and to show that you are interested in, care for, and yes, love, the speaker. As Sarah Young writes in *Jesus Calling,* "a renewed mind is presence focused."[v]

Notice that my listening wasn't passive. With other-focused listening, questions are a way to stay on the speaker's subject and learn more. Questions, good questions, also let the speaker know you are listening. The speaker knows the quality of your listening by the quality of your questions. More on questions in the next chapter.

Other-focused listening takes an enormous amount of self-control, especially when you know something about what the speaker is talking about. And isn't that the case 95% of the time?! Our friends, family and co-workers are most often coming to us *because* we have the topic in common. They might want to hear our opinion, **but not before we hear them out**. I constantly work to remind myself that I want to—need to—understand the unique thoughts and opinions of others rather than spending my time listening to my own stories in my head and hurrying to speak them. We'll come back to self-control later since it's easier said than done!

> The most basic and powerful way to connect to another person is to listen. Just listen. Perhaps the most important thing we ever give each other is our attention... A loving silence often has far more power to heal and to connect than the most well-intentioned words. *Rachel Naomi Remen*

I must confess, I love those long lunches with my girlfriends where we are all talking over each other, inserting our opinions on top of each other's. There is high energy and I feel so connected and affectionate towards them. Yet on the drive home, I realize that I didn't learn one new thing about them. I shared my thoughts, but I can revisit those anytime. I am left guilty and empty. I squandered an opportunity to demonstrate love and learn something new. Conversely, on the times when I've tried other-focused listening at my girlfriend gatherings, I learn a lot and go home energized, grateful, and like a worthy witness!

Now's a good time to tell you. I get it wrong. All. The.

Time. While I've been teaching the art of listening for twenty years, my husband still gets exasperated when he has to repeat himself or I interrupt him. We are talking about sanctification here, becoming more and more Christ-like. And we won't ever reach the goal this side of heaven. It's our journey—our quest—to become more like him, with the Holy Spirit as our guide. It's a worthy journey—the one God intends.

Oh, one more very important choice point. If your phone is in your hand or on the table (face up or face down), your body language is telling everyone within sight that you are in self-focused listening mode. A visible cell phone says you are "listening" for the sounds on your phone as much as you are listening to the other person. Choose to silence your phone, put it in your pocket or out of sight—and keep it there—if you want to give a sincere gift of other-focused listening.

4. Hyper-focused Listening

The ultimate way to listen is to so fully quiet your own emotions and thoughts, to be so present, that you can "hear" not only the speaker's words but the speaker's emotions and what's *not* being verbalized. When I choose this mode, I picture myself completely alone with the speaker. It's just him and me. The coffee shop recedes, and I visualize emptying myself of my thoughts and opinions. I am curious, wanting to soak up all the details, even the ones not spoken. In this mode, I am so present I can notice his eyes filling with tears, or the scrunched shoulders, or the heavy, hanging head. I am listening to the words so closely I can "hear" when he's leaving something out, or the sigh, or the whisper of the most important point.

Here's how it sounds.

Speaker: I'm overwhelmed at work.

Me: What's going on?

Speaker: Oh… there's so much to get done and never enough time. It's ok. I'm used to it.

Me: It doesn't look "ok." You look concerned. What's the heaviness I am sensing?

[by not taking his words at face value, I've given my friend permission to say more. I've let him know I genuinely want to listen to what's *really* going on.]

Speaker: The heaviness? [Silence. He's thinking. Trying to get clear for himself.]

(quietly) I think I'm a fraud. I didn't deserve this promotion.

Me: [Every fiber in my being wants to "fix" this. I want to yell, "You *totally* deserved this promotion!" But what love requires is to encourage my friend to process his thinking and emotions more fully before I share my own views.]

Those are powerful statements. There must be a lot of emotion behind them. What emotions are you grappling with?

Speaker: I'm not emotional about it. It's not *that* bad.

Me: Wow. If I thought I didn't deserve the promotion, I'd be feeling insecure, unworthy, maybe untethered. [I am helping him identify his emotions. He can use these suggested words to affirm or change his genuine feelings. I am giving him permission to "go there" with me. I'm letting him know it's safe to do so. And I am not hijacking the conversation with, "Whoa, I remember when I felt like a fraud at work! I had the worst boss ever! I didn't know what to do……"]

Speaker: Yeah, insecure is right. Useless. Not the sharpest knife in the drawer. I'm not sure what to do…

Me: [sounds like he's asking for advice, doesn't it? Resist the urge. You can't fully know the situation, his internal thoughts and emotions, or the details of what's going on. The loving move is to stay with his thinking; help him solve his problem himself since he's the expert in him!] What do you *want* to do?

Speaker: What DO I want to do?

This mode of listening is the most self-less and sacred of them all. It takes practice, humility and self-control (your cell phone is nowhere near you). If the Holy Spirit helps you see emotion in your speaker, the most loving act you can do is to choose hyper-focused listening. This is the realm of excellent counselors and life coaches, yet you can achieve it, too. We can't be a substitute for a licensed counselor, but we can show love with *the gift of attention and time.* Silence is golden when listening to a speaker expressing deep emotion. Consider someone who has just lost a friend or relative to death. Sitting with them in silence is a rare gift. We'll explore about the importance of silence and listening with the heart in later chapters.

Let's look back at God's description of love in I Cor 13 and see where this listening gift shows up.

> *Love is patient* [it waits to speak while listening well to another] *and kind* [focused on another, showing genuine interest in what they have to say]*; love does not envy or boast; it is not arrogant or rude* [self-focused listening is rude - hijacking a conversation and interrupting to hurry someone along is arrogant]. *It does not insist on its own way* [listening first and waiting for an appropriate time to share your thoughts and perspectives]

But What If…

As I promised you earlier, I want to address the objections any of us can have in giving the gift of listening to others.

As I noted at the beginning of this chapter, every time I teach these skills, there are two principal objections: this takes too much time and the talkers in life will take even *more* of my time.

One of the key reasons that people talk "too much" is that they believe that you are *Not Really Listening.* If your child is trying to tell you about the awful day she had at school and she sees a distracted look in your eyes or, worse, that you are scrolling through Instagram, or reading an email, she will **keep talking** until she believes you heard her. Yes, the *speaker* determines whether she thinks you are listening. Your body language speaks loudly, and the speaker will believe what she sees over a quick, "Yes, I'm listening!"

The way to make listening more efficient and **take less time** is to put your phone down, take your child to a quiet place, look her in the eyes and ask her to tell you about her awful day. Choose other-focused listening, and when emotions rise, choose hyper-focused listening. This works! Try it with your spouse, your co-worker, or the chatty neighbor. Honestly, people are so starved for quality listening that if they experience two to five minutes of your focused listening, they will feel authentically valued and loved.

"Come on, Elle! There are people in this world who will talk your ear off. I have one in my office. I'd get nothing done if I 'other-focused listened' to him!" Fair enough. Give this child of God five to ten minutes of hyper-focused listening (you can set your phone's timer) and then say, "I so appreciate you sharing that. I must honor my commitment to this deadline and get back to work." You will have been more Christ-like.

Another situation in which you will be tempted to ditch other-focused listening is when you are attentively listening to a friend, spouse or child and alarm bells are going off in your head. *If he does that, he'll fail! If she takes that step, she'll get hurt!* Be patient. Do not insist on your own way by hastily inserting, "No, you won't!". We'll address how to use quality questions in these circumstances in the next chapter.

Lastly, sometimes you can't realistically give your undivided attention. You are in the middle of folding a souffle or jumping on a virtual meeting. What does love require? If someone wants to talk to you and you must say "no" in order to say "yes" to another commitment, say something like: "I want to listen to you, and right now I can't. Could I find you in an hour when I can give you my full attention?" They will experience so much more love and respect when you follow up, than if you pretend to listen to them while your mind is elsewhere.

Listening to the Holy Spirit

> *The Friend, the Holy Spirit, whom the Father will send at my* [Jesus'] *request, will make everything plain to you. He will remind you of all the things I have told you. I'm leaving you well and whole. That's my parting gift to you.* (John 14:26 MSG)

Books have been written by theologians much smarter

than me on the Holy Spirit, and many of *you* could probably write this section for me. The following is my experience and how I envision God helping me answer the question, "What does love require of me?"

While I often yearn for clear "writing on the wall," I have never seen it. I do not always "hear" the Holy Spirit when I ask him a question. Sometimes I feel a nudge and sometimes it's silence, but taking that pause before engaging my Respond-ability is always worthwhile. At the least, I am slowing down my response long enough to tap into the exquisite brain God provided me. He has taught me many things over the years through his Word, pastors, teachers and friends. When I whisper to the Holy Spirit, "What does love require?" I am proceeding in peace instead of acting out of instinct or fear. By listening for His response or prompting, I can learn what the Spirit desires of me in that moment.

What Happens When I Listen?

Well before I learned Andy Stanley's thought-provoking question, I was sitting at the gate area for a flight and as I took my eyes off my phone, I noticed a young woman across the vast carpet, sitting in a crowded area crying. I had that strong nudge to go to her. *Oh, that's silly*, I thought. There were many people around her that God could call, although none were attending to her. "*Are you sure, God?*" I asked, hoping that maybe the nudge I'd felt hadn't really been from him. But he's always sure!

So, I got up, walked across about 100 feet of carpet and sat down in the chair—the only open chair—right next to her. "What's behind your tears?" I tenderly asked. She looked at me and immediately poured out that she was a nanny returning home to Europe and had just said goodbye to the little ones she had been caring for and living with for the past three years. She doubted that she'd ever see them again. I asked if I could give her a hug, listened a bit more and then, calling on my courage, I gently asked permission to pray for her. She said, "Yes."

That was it. So simple. Was it awkward? Yes. Did it make a difference? I think it did. It was what love required. Another human was crying in a public place, and everyone else either hadn't noticed or was trying to pretend they didn't. I am confident God sent me on that mission. What was the Holy Spirit's specific role? I imagine it was to raise my head and point out the young woman who was in obvious need. The Holy Spirit gave me that internal nudge, and I also know he gave me the courage to walk over and pray with her.

Another example of listening to the Holy Spirit occurred after I started teaching this curriculum at my church. During my 20 years as a consultant, I was a *frequent* traveler. Those of us in this category have potent preferences when in our traveling mode. One of mine is to not check my luggage. I've learned to pack a week's worth of professional clothes into a carry-on since every minute away from home is hard. I hate (yes, it's that strong) to wait at the luggage carousel and lose 30-60 more minutes before getting on my way.

So, there I was at the gate area after a long workweek, with my carry-on, and I was in Boarding Group 4. I was looking around assessing the competition. Would there be enough room in the overhead bins for my suitcase after First Class and three other boarding groups? When I arrived at the gate, 45 minutes early and aware of my "Four" rating, I got in the designated line and was first. This is how committed I am to carry-on. Instead of taking a comfortable seat for those 45 minutes, I was sitting on the floor in that narrow, roped-off lane (Can you picture me?)

As Boarding Group One was being called, the gate agent announced she would check all carry-ons for Group Four. What?! I didn't even get to play the game of wishing, hoping and praying that there would be room for mine? In all my years of traveling, I'd never had this happen. Usually, the agent would get a call from the flight attendants when things were full and then start checking them. I watched many roller-bags go by from my position at the front of Boarding Row 4. As I pulled mine up and handed my ticket to the agent, she told me she was going to tag my bag.

"Could I please see if there's room on-board first?" I asked kindly yet assertively. "No," she replied firmly, as she took my bag, tagged it and put it behind her. (Are you still with me? I'm feeling my emotions rise just *writing* this!) Again, as a seasoned traveler, usually you take your tagged bag and leave it at the top of the jetway. Odd. I was not happy. Yes, I can get cranky.

I asked the smiling flight attendant at the door if there were still open bins for suitcases. He looked surprised and replied, "I think so," like they hadn't even started to worry about it. As I headed to my 17A seat (I love the aisle) I was seeing quite a few spots for suitcases. The three bins right over 17A were *completely* empty! As my blood pressure rose, I put my briefcase in my seat and headed back down the aisle. My suitcase was just being loaded onto the cart that goes down to the belly of the plane. I took it out and headed back to my seat. The flight attendant saw me, and I explained that there was room over my seat.

Whew! I had saved that precious time and was envisioning sitting in my living room with my husband debriefing my trip in just a few hours. I opened my phone to play solitaire as the boarding was finishing.

"Where's your suitcase?!" demanded a female voice. Standing in the aisle next to me was the gate agent and the flight attendant. Shocked and defensive, no nerve in my brain was asking, "What does love require?"

I told her it was overhead. "Give it to me!" she snarled, and off she went with my suitcase! I was stunned. Speechless. Thank you, Holy Spirit. I somehow remembered to close my shocked mouth.

Did the flight attendant turn me in, I wondered suspiciously? I needed to do something. *This is outrageous!* I thought. And then that still small voice reminded me, "What does love require?" Ugh! Honestly, now?? I paused, pondered the question again, and sat back in my seat. The Holy Spirit had saved me from making a very non-Christian spectacle of myself. Thank you, Lord.

Now the emotions didn't miraculously retreat. I was still indignant, but I was listening with my heart and calming down. What *does* love require? I sat with that question as the door was closed. We taxied, the safety announcements were delivered, and we took off. It wasn't until they brought out the drink cart that I had an answer. The flight attendant made it slowly down to 17A and asked what I wanted to drink. I answered and then added in the gentlest tone I could muster, "What happened with my bag?"

"That was awful, wasn't it? I'm so sorry!" she responded. "I helped three people bring their bags on after you. I don't know what that gate agent was thinking, but you should write your experience on the Customer Service survey. You get those, don't you?" "I do," I answered. "I will try to get her name for you," she continued, "so you can specifically mention it. That shouldn't happen!"

Just like that empathy! And a reasonable solution to an injustice. She heard me. I didn't embarrass myself. I was a much better witness than I would have been on my own. Later in the flight, the two people next to me who had witnessed it all, weighed in with similar empathy. "I'm sure your bag will be off early," they assured me. Again, I was struck with what they might have thought/said if I had gone with instinct over the Holy Spirit. Or where the gate agent might have sent my bag!

How do you listen to the Holy Spirit? It's in that gap, the one Frankl[vi] described.

> *Between stimulus and response, there is space. In that space is our power to choose our response* [after asking the Holy Spirit for help]. *In our response lies our growth and our freedom* [in Christ].

You need to be in hyper-focused listening mode to "hear" the Holy Spirit. In that moment on the plane when I asked, "What does love require?" everything shut down around me. I was in a cone of silence. I didn't even know I had seatmates until the entire event was over. In that silence you may sense a still small voice, get a nudge, have an awareness in your heart, or use your God-given mind, but I promise you, you will grow and experience freedom. I felt such joy for the rest of that flight—even though my bag was in the plane's belly. Miraculously, my bag was on the carousel as I approached baggage claim.

Oh, friends, listening matters in our noisy, bustling world. God wants us to listen meaningfully to the needs, struggles, and perspectives of the people he puts in our paths. Even as little as two minutes of other-focused listening is more than most people get in a week and will be received as pure selfless love. Quality listening is a foundational gift of love that we will continue to return to as we build skills to *serve others humbly with love.*

Self-reflection

1. What has been your communication experience with the Holy Spirit?

2. When did you last use other-focused listening? What was the impact on the speaker? On you?

3. When you are *self-focused* listening, does your mind go on a journey of thought or do you interrupt and speak what's on your mind?

Exercises

1. Read Colossians 1:9-14. What phrase did God lay on your heart?

2. Who in your life needs the gift of listening? Try other-focused listening with three different people. How long can you keep the focus on the speaker? Notice when your mind goes to self-

focused listening (trust me, it will!) What worked well? Where did you stumble? Practice makes (more) perfect. Welcome to a lifelong growth opportunity!

3. Ask the Holy Spirit, "What does love require?" in the middle of your everyday life; while in line at the grocery store, at coffee with a friend, when your spouse comes home from work, etc. What happened?

Additional Reading

- *Active Listening 101: How to Turn Down Your Volume to Turn Up Your Communication Skills*, Emilia Hardman. 2012
- *Power Listening: Mastering the Most Critical Business Skill of All*, Bernard T. Ferrari. 2012, Portfolio

CHAPTER THREE

THE GIFT OF ASKING

My dear brothers and sisters, take note of this: Everyone should be quick to listen, **slow to speak** *and slow to become angry.* (James 1:19 NIV)

Even when we are using other-focused listening there can be a temptation to leap too soon to expressing our own opinion or perspective on the topic raised. What began as other-focused listening can soon look like a game of Ping pong—his opinion, your opinion, his opinion, your opinion, which can easily digress into self-focused listening. How do we avoid this?

James 1:19 gives us the answer, and the Amplified translation provides us additional insight: "Let everyone be quick to hear [be a careful, thoughtful listener], and slow to speak [a speaker of carefully chosen words]…"

We are told to be quick to listen **and then** slow to speak by using carefully chosen words. In the previous chapter, we learned how to be a thoughtful, active, other-focused listener. Now we need an additional skill—something that will help us slow our speech down. This important skill is another way we take that momentary pause and make the choice to *love well.*

Listen Then Ask

Slowing down our speech is best accomplished through learning how to ask good questions. Asking at least one question *before* sharing your opinion lets the speaker know you are truly focused on him—not just "waiting to speak" as the late comedienne, Joan Rivers defined listening. Your question, if it's a careful one, communicates that you are sincerely curious about what your friend has shared. It shows that you want to be sure you understand his thoughts, or you wish to go deeper into his thoughts before jumping to yours.

To stay focused on another person's perspective before giving yours takes *compassion, kindness, humility, gentleness and patience.* (Colossians 3:10 NIV) It is truly *serving one another humbly in love.* (Galatians 5:14 NIV)

Let's look at an example from our role model, Jesus, who was so skilled at asking good questions.

As Jesus approached Jericho, a blind man was sitting by the roadside begging. When he heard the crowd going by, he asked what was happening. They told him, "Jesus of Nazareth is passing by." He called out, "Jesus, Son of David, have mercy on me!"... Jesus stopped and ordered the man to be brought to him. When he came near, Jesus asked him, **"What do you want me to do for you?"** *"Lord, I want to see," he replied. Jesus said to him, "Receive your sight; your faith has healed you."* (Luke 18: 35-43 NIV, emphasis mine)

Crafting Careful Questions

Asking good questions is a skill anyone can master with intentional practice. Let's investigate the best tips for asking good, loving questions, most of which Jesus exhibited in his question to the blind man.

1. Use "What?" or "How?"

Asking your friend open-ended questions that begin with the words *what* or *how* allows more "space" for the answer. For instance, Jesus could have asked, "Would you like help to get somewhere?" or "Do you need money?" But in doing so, he would have limited the blind man's options. He would also have been inserting his own assumptions about what he thought the blind man wanted. Instead, Jesus asked an open-ended question so as not to bias the answer. And while *Jesus* may not have been surprised at the answer, I often am. I *think* I know where a person is going with a story, so I insert my own assumptions or guesses and provide one or two choices to the person. But when I pause and rephrase my question as an open-ended one (one that is not a choice of two options and seeks more than a "yes" or "no" answer), I learn so much more about someone. Jesus asked a great open-ended question that so lovingly gave responsibility and freedom to the blind man. "What do you want me to do for you?" Simple. Kind. It was attentive to the man's needs and desires. You will see more examples of what and how questions below.

2. Use other-focused listening

When you have shut down your own "tapes" on a subject and are listening for the speaker's unique perspective, you are best able to hear a word or concept that you'd like the speaker to expand on. Using the last word the person says is often a good way to keep her sharing and learn more.

Examples:

- **Speaker**: "I'm honestly concerned." **Listener**: "You said you were 'concerned'. What are your other concerns?"

- **Speaker**: "I recently had a significant conversation with my son." **Listener**: "What made it significant?"

- **Speaker**: "So I am thinking of doing just that!" **Listener**: "I've never considered looking at it like that. What do you see as the key benefits? Key costs?"

- **Speaker**: "I'm worried my girlfriend doesn't think I have the courage to do the right thing." **Listener**: "What is the 'right thing'?"

3. Use hyper-focused listening

When emotion is swirling and thinking is blurred, it is especially loving to stay on the person's topic and help her gain more clarity. Listen for the emotion behind her words and then ask about what you think you've heard. Or, ask about something the person is *not* saying that, if said, would move the discussion forward.

Examples:

- "You seem especially sad. [You've let him know you 'heard' the emotion under his words] How would you describe your emotions?" "What's behind the sadness?"

- "You're practically jumping out of your skin! What are you most excited about?"

- "When you were talking about your concerns, I felt like there was something that you left unsaid. What else is on your heart? What is the deeper concern?"

Bringing an unspoken emotion to the surface through a good question can often help move a discussion forward and encourage your friend to explore and own her emotions.

4. Avoid asking "Why?"

"Why" questions often elicit a sense of having to justify one's answer which can put a person on the defensive. For instance, in the last set of examples, I might be tempted to ask, "Why are you sad?" But when I begin with "why", the person may feel like I do not think she *should* be sad, or like she has to tell me something *really* sad to have me believe her emotion. She's more likely to think, "Am I justified in my sadness? Do I have enough data/facts to prove I am really sad?"

Do you see how my why question has unintentionally put my friend on the defensive? Now, instead of moving our conversation forward, I may have just shut it down.

Instead, you can change any "Why" question to a "What" or "How" question.

Examples:

- "What's behind the sadness?"
- "How does being overwhelmed at work show up at home?"
- "What's behind the tears?"
- "What's the greatest weight?"
- "How does this excitement compare to other joys in your life?"

5. Ask non-judgmental questions

I've mentioned this above in the discussion of "why" questions, but this point expands to more than just avoiding certain kinds of questions. The goal here is to express authentic curiosity in your questions rather than judgment, however unintentional that judgment may be. Stephen Covey's fifth habit in *7 Habits of Highly Effective People*[vii] comes to mind: "Seek first to understand *then* to be understood." That humble approach is the key to other-focused listening and brilliant questions.

Tone of voice is just as important as our word choice in determining whether people will perceive our questions as curious versus judgmental. Try this little exercise. Think of all the ways you can say: "What made you do that?"

Try emphasizing different words, use a gentle tone, a harsh tone, a mocking tone. Add a sigh right before you ask the question. Do you see how your tone makes all the difference in how your words are received?

6. Ask short, simple questions

A brief question will be more focused, easier for the speaker to answer, and it will be less likely to be perceived as judgmental. Jesus' question to the blind man was brief, simple, and to the point. When we get into long questions, we often end up inserting our own biases and judgments.

Examples of short, simple questions:

- "What else?"
- "What's most important?"
- "What's at the core?"
- "What emotions are coming up?" (I prefer this to the overused, "How does that make you feel?")
- "How can you get a different result?"

7. Ask questions that promote personal exploration

We want to ask questions to help deepen the speaker's thinking rather than questions that seek more facts so that *we* can solve the speaker's problem for him. Solving it for him is not as useful or caring. Our most loving move is to keep the discussion on the speaker's topic and ask thought-provoking questions that help the *speaker* think deeper and differently so *he* can solve the problem himself—he's the expert on him! You are not. Jesus did this for the blind man mentioned above. Jesus, who already knew everything about this man, took the time to ask a question that allowed the man to reveal his own needs and desires. He role-modeled a truly love-centered interchange.

The following story is an example of how to incorporate questions that help a speaker come to her own conclusion. It was an excellent lesson for me, and reminds me, even today, to always ask questions that help someone deepen their own thinking.

I was coaching an executive, and we were on our seventh session. In Executive Coaching, the client brings the agenda or topic to each session. In sessions one through six, we had been focused on his goals of being more effective with his co-workers. But in session seven, I asked him what he wanted to focus on, and he said, "I want to decide if I should ask my girlfriend to marry me."

Now, I am well trained to keep my body language neutral and non-judgmental, but I was really having to work at it this time. In my head, I wondered if it was even appropriate for me to work with my client in such a personal arena. I quickly remembered that coaching is about the "whole person" and this would certainly affect everything in his life from now on.

Did I want to be responsible for gathering data and then telling him the correct answer? Absolutely not! My job was to ask stimulating questions so that *he* could take all that he knew about himself, his girlfriend and their relationship, add the new thinking our conversation was sparking in him, and let *him* decide. Honestly, as he answered my questions all I could think of was, "*Don't ask her!!*" From what I was hearing it didn't seem like a smart move. But at the end of the hour, he decided he would ask her to marry him. Ten years and three children later, they're just fine.

There is certainly a place for mentorship, discipleship, and advice, but most often what love requires is being a careful guide for the individual so that she will **find her own path that will fit her personality, her circumstances, and her relationships**—none of which you know, and she does. Keep in mind that whatever topic a speaker brings up to talk about has likely been on her mind for a while. She's processed as much as she can on her own. Your contribution, your gift, is to help her get beyond her default answers and examine the issue in a different light.

You want to ask questions that deepen the speaker's

thinking, and help her become a stronger problem-solver— rather than you *being* the problem solver.

8. Ask questions that reveal assumptions

Often, we confuse truth with assumptions. People can struggle with another person or a situation and believe they're dealing with facts, but those "facts" might actually be assumptions that may be completely false. We'll spend more time on this in the next chapter when we examine the source of our assumptions.

Examples of ways to uncover facts and assumptions for others and yourself:

- "What do you know to be true?"
- "What's another way to explain that?"
- "What are you assuming?"
- "What do you think will happen if you choose [action they're proposing]"?
- "What do you think will be the benefits? The costs?"

Helping someone distinguish between assumptions and facts propels them to better decision-making.

Building Character and Wisdom

When children are little, you have to be their problem-solver. They do not have enough life experience to choose wisely, so you tell them (order them) not to touch a hot stove or run across a street. By the time they are in middle school, you want them growing in their own problem-solving skills and making the best choices and decisions when you're not there to tell them what to choose. Asking questions with the guidelines above will help them grow into wise, independent thinkers.

This example illustrates the concept, and you will see that it applies not only to child-rearing but to loving others enough to want them to be wise, independent thinkers.

A peer in my coach certification program told us how she used her new inquiry skills with her daughter, Fatima, a junior in high school. Fatima came home very excited one day and told her mom that she and her boyfriend, Nathan, had booked a hotel room for junior prom. You can imagine the self-control that Mom used to appear non-judgmental!

"Oh," she replied calmly and in her most neutral tone of voice, "What went into your thinking?"

"We won't have to drive home at 1 a.m. when all the drunk drivers are out! And we'll be super tired. We don't want to risk falling asleep at the wheel like Kyle did last year."

"Good thinking!" my wise friend replied. "Let's look at this from some other perspectives. What assumptions might Nathan make about being in a hotel room with you?" [She's getting her daughter to do some evaluation rather than telling her] "What rumors might result from you two sharing a room?"

A rich, thoughtful discussion ensued where some decision-making muscles were built for the future.

> You cannot teach a man anything. You can only help him discover it within himself. GALILEO

Lean into the Holy Spirit for Ideas

My favorite memory of the Holy Spirit coming to my rescue with good questions happened with another coaching client. She had mentioned in a few of our early sessions that she had been in a Christian sorority in college and that she had met her husband at church. Coaching ethics allows us to reference a client's faith if the client introduces it. Although she hadn't mentioned it again in our subsequent sessions, I had made a mental note of it. As my client was telling me the issue she wanted to wrestle with in the current session, that still small voice said, "Ask her what God wants her to do." I foolishly went into argument mode with the Holy Spirit, *"I can't ask that! I'm in a federal office building! That's not allowed!"*

"Ask her what God wants her to do," I heard again. Of course, in conducting this argument in my head and heart, I reverted to self-focused listening and lost some of my client's words. I turned back to other-focused listening while sensing it a third time, *"Ask her what God wants her to do."* When God repeats himself three times, I know it's him. At her next pause I cautiously said, "What does God want you to do?" Her face broke out in a big smile. "I was hoping you'd ask that!" she said

enthusiastically.

Obediently listening to the Holy Spirit meant I had the perfect question for my client at the perfect time.

Self-reflection

1. Which of the eight tips do you want to focus on growing?

    - Use "What?" or "How?" questions
    - Use other-focused listening
    - Use hyper-focused listening
    - Avoid asking "Why?"
    - Ask non-judgmental questions
    - Ask short, simple, questions
    - Ask questions that promote personal exploration
    - Ask questions that reveal assumptions

2. To whom could you give the gift of powerful questions?

3. What is your prayer regarding asking questions?

Additional Reading

- *Change Your Questions, Change Your Life: 12 Powerful Tools for Leadership, Coaching and Life,* Marilee Adams, Ph.D. 2016, Berrett-Koehler Publishers
- *Humble Inquiry: The Gentle Art of Asking Instead of Telling,* Edgar H. Schein. 2013, Berrett-Koehler Publishers, Inc.

Additional Reading

CHAPTER FOUR

WORDS AND IMPRESSIONS

Do not let any unwholesome [foul, profane, worthless, vulgar] words ever come out of your mouth, but only such speech as is good for building up others, according to the need and the occasion, so that it will be a blessing to those who hear [you speak]. (Ephesians 4:29 AMP)

Now it's your turn to speak! How do you do that with love? You've been quick to hear—using other-focused or hyper-focused listening skills—and slow to speak. You have kept the focus on the speaker by asking curious, non-judgmental questions. Now our goal is to continue to communicate *compassion, kindness, humility, gentleness and patience* while expressing our opinions and thoughts.

What We're Saying When We're Not Speaking

One way we "speak" that we often overlook is through body language. Experts tell us that more than half of our message is not what we *say*, but in what people *see* in our body posture and facial expressions[viii]. In fact, those experts tell us 55% of our communication is body language, 38% is tone of voice, and *only 7%* is our words. Seven percent. This means that over 90% of my communication is transmitted without actual words! It seems very important then to understand what body language is and how I can best use it to enhance my communication.

What types of body language typically say, "I love you" or "You are important to me"? For me, a sincere smile is the first and easiest way to communicate an open, loving attitude. A hand reaching out for a shake or open arms ready for a hug are other indicators that you are approachable and glad to see me.

Eye contact, which is an especially important type of body language in our American culture, can communicate that you are interested, trustworthy, or engaged. Conversely, lack of eye contact can evoke that you are insincere, disinterested, or that you lack integrity. In other cultures, eye contact is translated differently. It is important to know what facial expressions and body language say "You are loved and valued" in the culture in which you communicate.

How you hold your arms is another subtle body language message. Crossed arms may suggest you are closed to input or to that person. Holding your hands behind your back can communicate that you are hiding something or that you are shy. But drop your arms to your sides in a relaxed manner, and you've instantly revealed that you are **open to input**—similar to a Golden Retriever lying belly-up on the floor wagging her tail.

One last aspect of body language is not so much about our bodies but about how we choose to cover them. There was a very popular book written in 1975 and now updated called, *Dress for Success?*[ix] It was a best seller through the 1980s and *the* resource for how to make the best first impression. What we wear is part of the 55% of the message that people take in through their senses. So, ask yourself, "What does my clothing say about me? What assumptions might people make? What's written on my favorite t-shirt? On my tattoos?"

Carol Kinsey Goman writing in *Forbes Magazine*[x] explains what's at stake. "The moment [a person] sees you, his or her brain makes a thousand computations: Are you someone to approach or to avoid? Are you friend or foe? Do you have status and authority? Are you trustworthy, competent, likeable, confident? And we make these computations at lightning speed—making major decisions about one another in the first seven seconds of meeting."

Are those judgments and conclusions correct? Is it the truth about you? Maybe it is, and maybe it's not. You can't control other's thought process, but you *can* control the data you put in front of them and work to make sure that it's an accurate representation of who you are.

Recently a woman I passed on the street had a "loud" message on her shirt that simply read, "NOT SORRY!" Personally, that didn't leave me with the sense that she was approachable. On the other hand, I sense genuine warmth when I see a "Faith" t-shirt. Others might come to different conclusions. Actually, others *will* come to conclusions that differ from you. That's OK, and again, it's beyond our control. But what we *can* control is the consideration we put into communicating love even through what we choose to wear.

Body Language Matters

One drawback of body language is that it's not precise. When you see me frown, does it mean I am not happy to see you? That I'm sad or that I am confused about something I saw or heard? That I'm not well? If I do not add words to clarify what you see in my body language, my communication will confuse you and be less effective.

Another truth about body language is that it trumps words. Imagine that I am talking to you and telling you how happy I am to see you. I am frowning and my brow is scrunched together. My words are inconsistent with my body language, so now you have a choice to make. Will you decide that the truth is in what you see or in my words? You might seek clarity by asking me what is going on, since my frown doesn't match my happy words. Or if you do not know me well, you may choose not to say anything—but your trust in me has been taken down a notch. My words seem to contradict what you see. And we humans subconsciously trust body language over words as the truth. We believe body language doesn't lie.

Body Language Lessons

The first key to loving others well through our body language is to become more aware of what people see and, thus, assume about us. Though we can't control another person's perceptions of us, we can learn better body language choices that will enhance, support, and clarify our words for more authentic, cohesive communication.

How do people describe your body language or your presence? If you don't know, ask a close, trusted friend. Then consider and pray about what you could add to your unspoken language to speak love.

The second key is to check our own perceptions and assumptions about someone *else's* body language. A smile with eye contact and open body language makes me think you are warm and interested in me. I might even assume you are "safe" or trustworthy… unless I think your smile is inauthentic. An inauthentic smile immediately communicates to me you are not "safe". Could I be wrong in my assumptions? Absolutely! So, we need to know that we are making assumptions when we see body language and check them out. Questions are a great tool to clarify the body language we see. For example, "I see you're frowning. What's on your mind?"

We'll pause mid-chapter for a bit of reflection.

1. What body language or dress do you first notice in someone?

2. What do you see in others that "says" love or acceptance?

3. What three characteristics do you want people to assume about you in their first impression?

Finally! Using Our Words

Remember what the experts tell us. Our body language tells 55% of the story. Tone of voice adds another 38% and the actual words we say or write are the final 7% of our message.[xi]

When we speak, we share *our view of the world.* It's the only perspective we have, and we often assume it's right. Speaking can put us in a self-focused place, sometimes to an extreme where we think everyone sees the world the same way we do. A rule that will always put you on the right side of love is to listen first (understand their perspective first), ask questions second (for a deeper understanding), and *then* speak or advocate your opinion.

Imagine how much more effective and wiser your words can be when you have tried to **understand the other person first.**

How We Develop Our Perspectives

To best appreciate our thinking process and the subsequent words that come out of our mouths, I want to introduce you to organizational psychologist Chris Argyris' "Ladder of Inference" model.[xii] We could also call it our process of interpretation. It explains so elegantly what goes on in our minds leading to what we say.

Picture a ladder with the rungs labeled:

Take Action
Adopt Beliefs
Draw Conclusions
Make Assumptions
Add Meaning
Select Data
All the Data

We start at the bottom of this ladder with All the Data. In any situation, any interpersonal encounter, there is an enormous data set. It includes *everything* that can be seen or heard, billions of pieces of information—too many for the human mind to process. So, our first act, going up the ladder, is to Select the Data that's important to us. We subconsciously choose what we think are the relevant bits of data based on similar situations in our past.

Climbing higher, we then Add Meaning to what we see; Make Assumptions based on our life experiences and come to a Conclusion. We have just formed our perspective on a situation. Other people, in the same situation, select different data on which to focus, add their own meaning, make their own assumptions and come to, possibly, a (very) different conclusion.

For example, when I am at the front of the training room, I pick up quickly on the yawns, eye rolls, smiles and nods. As a professional facilitator, that body language data is important to me. Then, since our brains work to make meaning of what we experience with our senses, I add meaning to what I see or hear. The meaning I may add to the yawn is that she's bored; the eye roll, that he disagrees with the discussion direction or the topic; the smile or nod, that she agrees with the last point or appreciates the way I facilitate.

We continue to "run up our Ladder of Inference" as we Draw Conclusions, Adopt Beliefs, and finally, Take

Action which is often through voicing our "ladder"—our personal perspective. Other actions we take, often subconsciously, are through our body language. Some "loud" body language might include throwing down a pencil, crossing our arms, a high five, a dramatic sigh, frowning or smiling. Those wordless messages are the actions we take based on the conclusions we've come to.

Will the action I take be based on the full truth of the situation? Not likely. The yawn I took for boredom could mean, instead, that the person was up all night with a sick child or took a sleep-inducing cold medication that morning. The eye roll that I have concluded is a negative statement on the discussion could have instead, been in response to something else in the room—or in his head. The smiles and nods could likewise have many meanings. Even words can have different meanings to each individual present.

All that I process, illustrated on the ladder, is through the lens of my personal life experiences. I select what I think/believe is relevant data based on past incidents with the same data, and that is often very different from what others have selected to focused on.

An example of this happened several years ago when my husband, son, and I were driving through a beach community. We were all quietly looking out the window at the same (large) pool of data when my husband said, "That's interesting!" and my son said, "It sure is!" and I chimed in with "Yes!" Then it occurred to me. I should check to be sure I understood their perspectives correctly.

"What's interesting, David?" (A question to check my assumptions.) My husband, the driver, had noticed all the police cars out on the streets.

"Evan, what interested you"? He had noticed the many bike riders, which reflects his interests and therefore the data he selected.

And I had (only) noticed all the For Sale signs in the yards. I'm fascinated by real estate!

We had all been exposed to the same body of data, but had chosen vastly different things on which to focus. If I hadn't questioned Dave's comment, we each would have been left with the false belief that the others were looking at and fascinated by the same things we were! I realized I hadn't "seen" even one bike or police car!

Who spoke the "truth" of what was out our windows? All of us did! Each of us had one perspective on a vast array of data. This example not only establishes how we can reach a different but equally accurate perception as someone else, but it helps us appreciate God's ability to see everything perfectly all at once. Only he sees the whole picture. **We never can.**

When we come to a *conclusion* on our ladder, we assume it's truth. I am a smart person. When I see or hear something I assume I know what they mean. How could my conclusion not be true? Would it be true that the person who yawned was bored and shouldn't have been invited to the meeting? Would it be true that the eye-roller disagreed with our topic and is likely a difficult co-worker? No! Not necessarily.

Five Key Points from Ladder of Inference

1. **We are always selecting data and NEVER have all the data.**

What love requires is for us to inquire about what others saw/ heard (the data they selected) and add it to the data or facts we selected *before* we take action/speak. My family's drive through the beach community illustrates that. We will speak much more knowledgeably if we have the benefit of more eyes on more data—an expanded view, not just our limited perspective.

2. **We are always adding meaning and making assumptions.**

Remember that we naturally make assumptions and, therefore, we need to **check to determine if our assumptions are correct or false**.

I know a couple who got into an argument because the wife who ran the family's small business, said they needed to make a significant investment in the store. The husband, a pilot for a major airline, panicked and harsh words ensued until the husband took a pause to ***ask***, "What do you mean by 'significant' investment?" The answer: $10,000. This amount was 'significant' to the wife but not to the pilot who thinks of a 'significant' business investment in terms of millions of dollars. They had added completely different meanings to the simple word "significant," but it took the husband's question to reveal that to them.

3. **We should always take advantage of a Holy Spirit pause before we speak.**

If we jump to action and speak before checking our thinking, we can often hurt someone or embarrass ourselves.

My son, Evan, who was in a full-time master's program at the time and had the subsequent debt, stopped by our house and told me he had bought pinwheels that day. I am sure you can imagine this mom running up her "ladder," and coming to the instant conclusion that he was terribly irresponsible. My action might have sounded like, "What on EARTH are you doing buying toys??!!!"

I caught myself that day as the Holy Spirit gave me an elbow to the side, and I paused to **ask a question** and check my assumptions. "Pinwheels?" I asked. It turned out that Evan had purchased fish filets topped with creamed spinach, rolled up and cut into 'pinwheels' from the day-old bin at Target! I gathered more information and clarity (seeking first to understand before I reacted) and adjusted my conclusion 180-degrees. He was suddenly such a responsible young man!

Another time the Holy Spirit guided me was when we were out to a late breakfast at IHOP. The server brusquely threw our menus on the table and grunted, "I'll be back to take your order." My mind flew up my "ladder" and I inwardly concluded that she was surly and disrespectful. Thankfully, I paused before I responded. I didn't take any immediate action with my body or words. I thought of a question to check my assumptions and conclusions. Picture me with a Superman Cape that says, "Respond-ability!"

When the server returned, I asked, "How early do you have to be here for work?"

"7:30."

Without the *thought* of a pause I responded, "Oh, that's not too bad."

"Yes. But it's the eight-month-old who's not sleeping and my three-year-old who was angry when I said I wanted to send the baby back."

Wow! I had new data that humbled me and totally changed my conclusion. She wasn't surly and disrespectful; she was an exhausted, defeated, hard-working mom who needed empathy and kindness. I shudder to think how I would have behaved (taken action) if, instead of checking my conclusion, I had continued up the ladder and responded with an eye roll or worse! That would have been the opposite of the witness I desire.

4. **When we adopt a belief, our tendency is to seek data that supports our belief in future situations.**

We reflexively, usually *unconsciously*, seek information or data that supports our way of thinking. So, once we Adopt a Belief, we are laser-focused on (only) the data that supports that belief. It explains stereotypes or bias. I will humbly illustrate.

I love breakfast so when I travel for work, I am down in the hotel restaurant quite early for my coffee, bacon and eggs. Picture me seated at one of those tiny tables for one. My coffee cup was empty. I like it hot and always finish it quickly before it cools. Eager for my second cup, I looked around for my server (uh-oh, is there a pattern here?)

I couldn't get her attention. Suddenly and *without taking a Holy Spirit pause* (my cape was back in the hotel room) I adopted a belief: *women who travel alone get no respect.* I am sure I had some data from the past that I was relying on and added to this situation, because it made perfect sense to me. *Women who travel alone get no respect.* (Say it with the authority of truth to follow me here!) I continued to scan the restaurant for proof. She was chatting with two men in suits a few tables over and then moved to the family of four. But she was totally ignoring me. My indignation was boiling over.

Finally, she came up to my table, smiled and asked, "Do you want more water?"

Are you kidding me?! It's 6:00 a.m.! I don't need water. I need coffee. I teach this stuff. So I took a pause to adjust my body language and tone of voice. I asked in my calmest, sweetest voice, "Actually, I'd like another cup of coffee."

Whereupon she picked up my **personal pot of coffee** from the tiny table and poured it for me! (Cue humiliation.) I had been so busy *gathering data to support my newly adopted belief* that I didn't see the pot of coffee On. My. Table.

I wonder what beliefs she has about women who travel alone! Yes, I was *very* generous with my tip.

The only way to control our stereotypes and biases is to pause and ask the Holy Spirit, "What am I missing here?" We have to consciously look for data to the contrary—contrary to the data we naturally gather to support our beliefs. I might have asked myself, "*What do I see or hear that makes me believe women who travel alone are* ***respected****?*" I would have had to take the time to more objectively look at my surroundings, and then perhaps I would have *seen the coffee pot on my table*! THEN my conclusion would have been: *I'm so respected and cared for by this server that she gave me my own pot!*

One of my class participants volunteered she had a "thankless job". She was ardent. "Really, NO ONE, ever says 'thank you' for what I do for them." I challenged her to look for data to the contrary; to count how many "Thank you's" she received during the next week. She pushed back. "I just told you. No one **ever** says that." She counted 17.

5. We are always making stories up in our head.

Our brains are amazing, God-designed computers, always trying to make sense of our world, select data from the vast pool of data available, assign meaning, and reach conclusions. It's how we were created.

This is one of the crazier stories I made up in my head as I ran up the Ladder of Inference. When I was deciding what college to attend, my parents suggested I look at the University of Colorado (locally known as CU). They encouraged me to see the world. A beloved aunt and uncle lived in the Denver area, so I would have them nearby if I got homesick. **I never looked** at materials from CU and never asked to go see it. I didn't need to; I concluded. I knew/made-up that *all* the students at CU were skilled downhill skiers. I had never skied. I obviously couldn't go there.

Do you hear my faulty Ladder? Was I making inferences and faulty interpretations? We need to remember to check the stories we tell ourselves. One way is simply to ask yourself, "What is another way to tell that story?"

Later, as a married mother of two, God moved us to Colorado. I took ski lessons at the age of 32 and am average on the slopes. I can't tell you how many native Coloradans and CU students have told me they've never skied! More data, more truth.

How We Can Do Better

Whenever we take action through our speech or body language, we need to remember that we are only advocating our **unique perspective, our point of view.** It's the only thing we have! **Jesus spoke absolute Truth**. But what we speak about is always filtered through our life experiences and our Ladder of Inference. We shouldn't *"insist on our own way"* (1 Cor 13:5 NIV) of thinking if we want to love others. We must listen to them and seek to understand their perspective.

This is hard work, my friends. But it is what love requires. It's accomplished with the power of the Holy Spirit. We can't do this on our own.

Three tips on speaking with *compassion, kindness, humility, gentleness and patience*

1. Walk your listener up or down your Ladder of Inference. Make your thinking pattern transparent.

   Up the Ladder: "The way I see it, I looked at these facts (my selected data), I assumed that (word) meant (this), and I concluded/decided ______________."

   Down the Ladder: "I think we should (my conclusion/opinion). I assumed that (my assumptions) and figured we meant (the meaning I added) when we said (specific word) and I focused mainly on (my selected data/facts)."

2. After walking them up or down your Ladder end with, "What am I missing?" You've shifted from sharing your perspective to a question. You communicate that you know you might not have all the data, or the right meanings or assumptions, and are open to hearing from the other party.

3. If you need to resolve a disagreement (someone else has a different conclusion/decision/opinion), ask questions to bring to light the data the other person selected. Check what meaning they added and what assumptions they made. It is in seeking first to understand specific "rungs on the ladder" (Select Data, Add Meaning, Make Assumptions) that **the most productive, kind conversation occurs, and we achieve quality resolutions**. More on this in the chapter on conflict.

Remember, the easiest formula for communicating with love is to listen first, ask questions second, and speak or advocate last.

> *And if anyone longs to be wise, ask God for wisdom, and he will give it! He won't see your lack of wisdom as an opportunity to scold you over your failures, but he will overwhelm your failures with his generous grace.* (James 1:5 TPT)

> The more you say, the less people remember.
> *Francois Fenelon*

Self-reflection

1. What concept about speaking resonates the most with you?

2. How do you want to change your speaking habits?

3. Ask the Holy Spirit to reveal some of your biases to you. How can you be more intentional about seeking data to the contrary?

Exercises

1. Think of a person about whom you have a strong, negative opinion. Next time you interact with him/her, look and listen for *the opposite.* If you believe they are dishonest, listen for any honest statement they make. If you have adopted the belief that they are lazy, look for a way in which they have stepped up, volunteered or hunkered down to work.

2. Next time you make a strong case for something, or advocate a decision, make your last sentence, "What am I missing?"

Additional Reading

- *Everyone Communicates, Few Connect: What the Most Effective People Do Differently*, by John C. Maxwell, 2010 Thomas Nelson
- *Fitly Spoken: Developing Effective Communication and Social Skills*, by Greg S. Baker. 2011, Brighton Publishing LLC

CHAPTER FIVE

THE LOST ART OF ACKNOWLEDGEMENT

Do not let any unwholesome talk come out of your mouths, but ***only what is helpful for building others up according to their needs****, that it may benefit those who listen.*
(Ephesians 4:29 NIV)

… And never let ugly or hateful words come from your mouth, but instead let your words become beautiful gifts that encourage others; do this by speaking words of grace to help them. (Ephesians 4:29 TPT)

Using our words to build others up is a *beautiful gift* of love. Choosing to give the people who God places in our paths a sense of being known and loved is a way for us to *build them up according to their needs.* It's a way to use our voice for blessing.

Choosing to love by acknowledging others is possibly the easiest of all the behaviors we'll discuss. As we daily clothe ourselves with *compassion, kindness, humility, gentleness and patience* (Col 3:10 NIV) the practices in this chapter are the shoes we slip on just as we leave the house. And you would never forget your shoes, would you?!

An acknowledgement can range from a simple, "Hello," or "Thank you," to speaking deep into someone's heart. It's about commending people for who they are; the precious, unique children God created.

I See You

When I traveled to South Africa on a mission trip, I learned that the everyday greeting there is "Sawubona." It's used like our "Hello," only more profound. "It literally means 'I see you, you are important to me and I value you'. It's a way to make the other person feel seen, and to accept them as they are with their virtues, nuances, and flaws. In response to this welcome, people usually say 'Shiboka', which means, 'I exist for you.'"[xiii] What a picture of love!

In our culture, besides saying, "Hello," we use our body language to make eye contact and smile, which says, "I see you. You are important to me." Choosing to acknowledge others with this simple practice is a gesture of love that we can sprinkle throughout our days like rain on dry crops.

Use Names

An important way to acknowledge the people God puts in your life is to learn and use their names. Our names are meaningful to us, and we feel known when people use them. Now, many of you may think, "I can't remember the names of people for the life of me!" I think we've all encountered that embarrassing situation where we get introduced to someone at a party or event and her name flies right by our ears. Ten minutes into a fascinating conversation with this new friend, and you can't remember her name! It's terribly awkward. I challenge you to step up your game in this area, and intentionally *choose* to learn names.

When meeting someone for the first time, look them in the eye when they say their name, and listen at a hyper-focused level. When I do this, I really look at them—see them. I try to associate something about them with their name. Maybe the Cecelia introduced to me wears her hair the same way as another "Cecelia" that I know, or the Evan sharing an Uber with me has the same close goatee as the other "Evan" I know. Or the Jim who has just been assigned to my project team wears the same flannel shirts as my good buddy, "Jim."

If it's an unusual name, I often ask the person to spell it so I can visualize it, or I read their nametag if they have one. I also use their name in the next sentence or two, to anchor it in my brain. For example, "Evan, where are you from?" "How long have you been coming to this church, Cecelia?"

In my work, my classes often involve spending three to five days with a new group of people. As I meet them that first morning, I *consciously choose* to learn the participants' names. When I am intentional, I find I can learn and retain about 40 names before that first lunch break. When I call each person by name as their hands go up with questions throughout the week, they feel known and valued. It makes a difference. And when I forget a name, I simply say, "I'm sorry. Can you tell me your name again? I want to get it right." That is so much more honoring than pretending to know it, but not using it!

Please and Thank You!

Another simple way to appreciate others and show gratitude for who they are is a specific "Thank you," along with honoring body language and tone of voice. I look for people every day who are *serving* **me** *humbly with love,* but who frequently do not feel seen. It blesses *me* to recognize them for what they contribute.

- To the janitor cleaning the public restroom, "Thank you for making this space so fresh."
- To the cashier who takes my drive-up food order or checks me out at a register. "Thank you for being so efficient and friendly."
- To the server clearing your table. "Thank you for taking such good care of us."

I recently had fun with this at Freddy's, my favorite fast-food restaurant. I leaned over the counter toward the folks who prepared my outstanding burgers and fries and exclaimed, "Thank you! You make the best burgers and fries on the planet!" The look on their astounded faces made my day, and I pray my action made them feel seen—known—and loved!

A kind "Thank you," is one way to choose love. What about "Please"?

- When a server asks if you want more water, you can grunt, nod or choose love and look them in the eyes while saying, "Yes, please. That would be great!"
- When getting a stranger's attention, "Please, sir!" is so much more loving than "Hey!"
- When requesting something we can say, "I'd like the back tire looked at," or choose, "Could you please look at my back tire?"

Perhaps it's just semantics. I'd argue that it gives dignity and value to the receiver. You let them know you see and appreciate their humble service. When you travel internationally, make sure you know at least "please" and "thank you" in the language of your host country.

Acknowledgment for Who They Are

A deeper way to acknowledge someone is to recognize the character traits they exhibit.

- "I saw your composure, patience and courage as you fielded those tough questions."
- "It took grace and kindness to handle that last customer."

- "I noticed you invested your heart and mind in studying tonight. I so appreciate your perseverance and integrity."

Or let them know you see them living out their core values. More on core values in Values, Vulnerability and Trust ahead.

- "You are a role-model to me in how you honor your value of family."
- "Your honesty and authenticity were in full display at Bible study today."
- "I know respect is important to you. I loved how you showed it to that homeless person."

Envision the look on Zacchaeus' face, an outcast in a Bible story, when he heard his savior say:

> *"Zacchaeus, hurry and come down, for today I must stay at your house."… Jesus said to him, "Today salvation has come to this household, because he, too, is a [spiritual] son of Abraham."* (Luke 19:5, 9 AMP)

Or the glisten in the eyes of the children when Jesus warned:

> *Watch that you don't treat a single one of these childlike believers arrogantly. You realize, don't you, that their personal*

angels are constantly in touch with my Father in heaven? (Matthew 18: 10 MSG)

Common Courtesy

Other simple ways we can choose to reflect Christ's love are:

- Holding the door for someone.
- Giving up your seat on a bus, shuttle, or train.
- Giving a brief wave with eye contact when a car stops for you to cross in the pedestrian lane.
- Letting someone go in front of you in line.
- Giving a wave when merging in traffic.
- When needing help, choose to ask the person least like you. It usually surprises the person and lifts them up at the same time.
- What else comes to mind?

> Noticing and being present to appreciate people creates a feeling of gratitude and positivity. Being genuinely curious and a constant learner adds to the skills of honoring the self and others.
>
> *Prabha Chandrasekhar*

Cancel Culture

If making people feel seen and appreciated—known and loved—is a godly gift to them, then today's cancel culture is Satan's gift of hate. Wikipedia defines cancel culture as "a modern form of ostracism in which someone is thrust out of social or professional circles either online on social media, in the real world, or both."[xiv] It's a way to hate—rather than love—your enemies by attempting to wipe their memory off the face of the earth and punish them through a ruined reputation. "Cancelling" people is an intentional effort to make them feel fully *un*known and *un*loved.

We make an enormous impact for Christ when we intentionally provide the opposite experience—creating an experience of being known and loved. With our written and spoken words, we can embrace people with acceptance and love. We can change our culture by simply calling forth the brilliance, beauty, and value we see in every person who crosses our paths. We can choose to respond with grace to those who cancel others. Loving one another is something we can do in every moment. And every time you do, Jesus smiles and whispers, "Well done, good and faithful servant."

Self-reflection

1. How do you like to be acknowledged by friends?

2. Which acknowledgement practice do you want to make a new habit?

3. Ask the Holy Spirit who in your life needs more acknowledgement.

Exercises

1. Sprinkle sincere gratitude to others throughout your day tomorrow. Notice the impact on the person it's directed to, and the effect on you.

2. Ask God to show you one person each day to acknowledge for their character or core values.

CHAPTER SIX

A BALANCING ACT

We've explored three modes of communication: listening, asking, and speaking. The best communicators use these modes correctly, lovingly and in a balanced way, fluidly moving between asking, listening and speaking. They spend equal time in each[xv] while being mindful of their body language and tone of voice. This balance is an art that takes intentional practice to do well.

Unfortunately, we overuse the communication mode with which God has especially gifted us. We may do this unconsciously, but if we want balanced, effective communication that honors others above ourselves, we have to stop using one mode more than the other two. We can boost our love quotient in our everyday conversations if we simply raise our self-awareness in this area and make a commitment to practice the modes of communication in which we are less adept.

Creating Balance—I Can't Stop Talking

I like to speak and am comfortable speaking in front of 40 or 400 people. I teach a full range of communication skills, from how to give one-on-one feedback to how to give testimony before Congress. My preference for extroversion on the Myers-Briggs Type Indicator,[xvi] a well-known personality assessment, means I do my thinking and processing out loud. I feel an *obligation* to fill silences and am often the first to raise my hand whenever a question is asked in a class. Anyone with me?

While this preference for speaking serves me well, it can also hinder me. I can get "stuck" in a talking mode. I beat myself up after a lunch with a friend because I realize, too late, that I did all the chatting.

We need to be self-aware of our default or preferred mode of communication so that we can recognize when we should **step out of that mode.** In my case, to stop talking and add asking and listening to the conversation. I *want* to hear other people's perspectives and opinions. I just get on a roll of transmitting!

While it is mostly **my personal responsibility** to catch myself talking too much, most of us who default to speaking *do not mind at all* if you kindly help us out. "Elle, that's an interesting perspective. Cynthia, what are you thinking?" Even, "Thanks, Elle, let's hear from some others." Every time someone has had the courage to do this, I've been so grateful. Thank you for saving me from myself! It's what love requires.

Creating Balance—I Can't Stop Listening

Others, like my wise husband, prefer to lead with listening. It's almost a superpower. He will listen to everyone else's opinion in a meeting and then, at just the right time, he speaks, and it's frequently a perfect synthesis and solution to the problem! Often, though not always, those who default to listening have a preference for introversion on the Myers-Briggs Type Indicator.[xvii] They prefer to process internally and *then* speak. Imagine that! Thinking *before* speaking! It's a lovely trait - and almost impossible for me. Yet, the same principle applies. Those who prefer a listening mode can find themselves "stuck" there and need to step out of it into asking or speaking *sooner rather than later*. My husband tells me he prefers about five to ten seconds of silence before he steps into a conversation. Again, a lovely quality. But in a room full of extroverts that rarely happens.

While it is mostly the listeners' responsibility to catch themselves listening too much and shift to speaking or asking, those of you who prefer listening *rarely mind at all* if we kindly help you out.

"Courtney, we haven't heard from you. What do you think?" Giving the listener a heads up is even better. "Ethan, after we hear from Calvin (the one raising his hand wildly) I would love to hear from you."

Every time someone has had the courage to do this, the *room* has been so grateful. The rest of us haven't taken the time to notice that Courtney and Ethan haven't spoken—we are too busy talking and they seem so happy to just be listening! Since the listeners in the room have been quietly processing all that is articulated, they often have an intelligent perspective that moves the discussion forward. If you prefer the listening mode, please do not withhold this wisdom from us!

Creating Balance—I Can't Stop Asking

I have found in my work across the country that fewer people default to or are skilled at the asking mode. Questions move a discussion forward and prevent us talkers from monopolizing the conversation. Whenever you find yourself stuck in listening or speaking, consider asking a well-placed, open-ended question to put the exchange on a more productive path.

If you have a person in the conversation who leans too heavily on questions, simply invite him to step into a speaking mode, "Jordan, I'd love to hear what you think about this."

Creating Balance in a Discussion

One of my responsibilities as a professional facilitator is to guide a group in striking the right balance of communication. With the benefit of the Holy Spirit, all of us can serve a group of friends, co-workers or children by humbly and with love interjecting some helpful questions or phrases to facilitate a balanced discourse.

- **Invite a listener to speak**. "Preston, what do you think?"
- **Invite a speaker to listen**. "Cathryn, I hear your passion on the idea to __________. Let's hear from others."
- **Ask a question** to move the discussion forward. "Have we reached a consensus? What's the next step?"
- **Check in** to further the conversation. "I'm thinking we've gotten off-track. What are you noticing?"

Balancing the Various Forms of Communication

With in-person communication you have the full message: body language, tone of voice and the spoken words.[xviii] But in today's world we often find that we need to have important conversations through other means, or we want the convenience and efficiency of a quick text or email. When we use text, email and social media (unless it's video), the recipient is only getting 7% of your intended message. Just the words. Pause. Meditate on that. Only 7%.

We try to make up for this glaring communication deficit with emojis, but there is no sarcasm font. Unless we use ALL CAPITALS, we do not have any "tone of voice." And no emoji can fully communicate body language. So, 93% of the meaning of our texts and emails is left to the reader's interpretation and imagination. No wonder there is an overabundance of misunderstanding in our world of written communication. And no wonder I am compelled to use italics and bold in my book!

One consulting firm I work with has a Golden Rule that addresses this "failure to communicate," (quoting the warden in the movie *Cool Hand Luke)*. When we sense rising emotion in ourselves or we think the other party may have potent emotions about the topic, we must **pick**

up the phone to at least add tone of voice to the conversation. We may start a discussion by text, but as we sense things heating up—or we feel misunderstood—we consciously and deliberately call the person. Adding deliberate, intentional voice to your communication is, at its heart, an act of love.

Virtual meetings like Zoom, Teams or FaceTime have become the norm in our telework environment. While you do add tone of voice with these formats, nothing takes the place of an in-person conversation where you have exceedingly more opportunity to pick up on subtle, important body language.

For the sake of communicating with love, **when it's a crucial, emotional, and/or potentially conflict-laden conversation, meet in person.** When that's not possible, use the phone, ideally Face Time or other video options.

A Balance in Prayer

Just as we can have an imbalance in our communication with others, we can also be imbalanced in our conversations with God. I will confess that I often do more asking than speaking or listening in my prayer time.

Talking to God

I am pretty good at telling God what I'd like to see happen in the future. This is incongruent since I know that God's plan is perfect, and I know I don't have all the "data" as he does. To regain congruency in my beliefs, I tell him what I want: to protect Presley, to heal Anna, to give my friend a specific new job *and then adding*, "if it be your will." That keeps me true to my faith in his perfect plan, and puts me in a position to look intentionally for his hand in the situation. It keeps me open to how *he chooses* to answer my prayer. Which may differ greatly from my "how"—but oh, so much better in the eternal scheme of things.

I am also learning to pray, or speak, God's promises rather than outline all the lengthy details of my problem. For instance, speaking these verses in prayer can soothe my soul far more than describing how I think God should solve my problem, and it keeps me focused on God rather than on my problem.

> *For He will hide me in His shelter in the day of trouble.* (Psalm 27:5 NIV)

> *The steadfast love of the LORD never ceases, his mercies never come to an end; they are new every morning; great is your*

> *faithfulness.* (Lamentations 3:22-23 NIV)

> *And my God will meet all your needs according to the riches of his glory in Christ Jesus.* (Philippians 4:19 NIV)

I suspect God would like us to add more speaking from the heart, as in the Psalms, to pour out our emotions, and tell him how concerned, angry, or ecstatic we are. I imagine he wants us to share details of our lives as we would with an earthbound friend and acknowledge when we've messed up, veered off course, or need forgiveness. There are a plethora of solid books on prayer, I am just connecting our exploration of speaking skills to our communication with God.

Asking of God

Most of us have this down. Since God is God, when we ask in faith, we can ask for anything, knowing that his answer may be "Yes," "No," or "Not yet."

> *Truly, I tell you, if you have faith as small as a* **mustard seed,** *you can say to this mountain, 'Move from here to there,' and it will move. Nothing will be impossible for you.* (Matthew 17:20 NIV)

> *You did not choose me, but I chose you and appointed you so that you might go and bear fruit—fruit that will last—and so*

> *that whatever you* ***ask in my name*** *the Father will give you.* (John 15:16 NIV)

> *You may* ***ask*** *me for anything* ***in my name****, and I will do it.* (John 14:14 NIV)

What if we used short "What" and "How" questions to God as we explored in The Gift of Asking chapter?

- What is my role in this [situation or current conflict with someone]?
- How do I need to grow to be more effective for you?
- What do you want me to do?
- What do you need me to learn?

Asking only yes/no/maybe questions limits God more than I desire. I am committed to adding more of these types of questions—and then listening.

Listening to God

I do not spend enough time in this mode. While I have encouraged us to pause before every response to listen to him, I also want to add quieter, longer periods of time to listen in my prayer time. If my husband seeks five-ten seconds of silence before he weighs in to a discussion, I suspect God desires at least that. I need time to still my heart and mute the tapes in my mind before I am even in the right posture to "hear" his words.

When our son and daughter-in-law told us they were starting the adoption process to bring a child from China into their family, our human brains didn't get it. They had student debt, were living in a 50-year-old house, surviving paycheck to paycheck, and their one-year-old daughter, our dear Eden, was not sleeping over three hours at a time. A Chinese adoption costs over $30,000. It just didn't add up for us.

For over a year I regularly prayed, God, *how can I be aligned with your will in this situation?*

Then one day our son told us they had been matched with a one-year-old boy who was recovering from open-heart surgery. They would fly to China within the year to bring him home. Sadly, my heart was not yet at peace so I continued to pray as I had been, *"Lord, how can I be aligned with your will?"*

About a week later, in the still of the night, I clearly heard, "This is Eden's brother." *I'm making that up in my head*, I thought, although that's not the way I would have phrased it. Then the message came again, "This is Eden's brother." *Could it be? Is that how I need to align my thinking?* And again, "This is Eden's brother." Instantly, I had my answer. My heart was aligned with the Lord's and was completely at peace. Our precious, smart, affectionate, made-in-China grandson came home that year and has blessed us continually for the last four years. He has inspired us as we watched him bravely face two more open-heart surgeries here in the States. Thank you, God, for my own "heart surgery".

Lectio Divina is another prayer practice that I find useful to hear from God through his Word. I've heard it described as reading scripture with the "ear of the heart." There are many wonderful Lectio Divina resources available on the Internet. My favorite is from a website called Prayer and Possibilities[xix]. This prayer method is simple and profound and is a wonderful exercise to build heart listening skills. Here is the process.

1. **Read** a passage of scripture. Not as long as a full chapter. A few verses work well.
2. **Read** it a second time. Put yourself in the story.
3. **Read** it a third time, listening with your heart open to the Holy Spirit.
4. **Reflect** on the word or phrase that caught your attention.
5. **Respond** in prayer to that word or phrase.

6. **Rest** in God. Contemplate his Word to you.

Appropriately balancing our communication is a loving act in any conversation. When we choose to spend less time in our default mode (speaking for me) and more time in the others (listening and asking for me) we enrich our relationships. People feel heard, valued, and loved after our interactions with them.

Self-reflection

> *Be on your guard; stand firm in the faith; be courageous; be strong. Do everything in love.* (I Corinthians 16:13-14 NIV)

1. What do you have to guard against as you learn how to communicate with love?

2. What will take courage and strength to improve your communication?

3. What communication skill is easy for you, and which do you want to enhance?

4. What change can you make in your conversations with God?

Additional Reading

- *Crucial Conversations*, Kerry Patterson, et al. 2002, McGraw-Hill

CHAPTER SEVEN

MORE EQ, PLEASE

To love people well when we are communicating takes self-control. We need to control our desire to speak instead of listen, control how we use our excess brain capacity when we are listening, and control our tendency to use one mode of communication over the others.

Self-control, a fruit of the Spirit, is at the heart of what we now call emotional intelligence, or EQ. EQ is the science behind the fruit of the Spirit (love, joy, peace, patience, kindness, goodness, faithfulness, gentleness and self-control Gal 5:22-23 ESV). I love when research catches up with the Word of God! So, what is EQ?

We all know smart people, people with what we call high IQ or Intelligence Quotient. They get straight A's in school and often move up quickly in their chosen professions. But some do not. Not all smart people are "successful."

In the 1990s, researchers looked for the missing piece. Why did some straight A students struggle in their careers and some average C students who didn't choose to go to college succeed wildly? These researchers believed there was more to "success" than IQ. Professors Peter Salovey and John D. Mayer named this additional success factor Emotional Intelligence or EQ. According to Salovey, currently President of Yale University, and the Chris Argyris Professor of Psychology, and Mayer, Professor of Psychology at the University of New Hampshire, EQ is "a form of social intelligence that involves the ability to monitor one's own and others' feelings and emotions, to discriminate among them, and to use this information to guide one's thinking and action". Psychologist and science journalist, Daniel Goleman, author of *Emotional Intelligence: Why it can matter more than IQ.*[xx], made their work popular. Today there are over 6,000 books on the topic and multiple assessments you can take to determine your level of EQ.

The Four Emotional Intelligence (EQ) Elements

The first two elements, or skills, involve your observations—what you "see" or recognize in yourself and others.

1. **Self-Awareness** is your ability to perceive accurately your own emotions and appreciate the typical reactions you have to specific events, challenges and people. Someone with higher EQ will be more attuned to his emotions and is conscious of events, situations and people that cause him to have heightened emotion.

2. **Social Awareness** involves your ability to read *other people's* emotions accurately, assess what others are thinking and feeling and understand others' perspectives. Someone who is *low* in EQ is less able to connect body language to emotions and is more likely to think everyone has the same perspective as she does.

The next skill is about what action(s) you choose to take or not take based on what you have perceived or seen. It is self-control in action. This is where you will want to engage your Respond-ability Superpower.

3. **Self-Expression** is your **action or lack of action** when you experience emotions, coupled with your ability to manage yourself and your behavior appropriately (self-control). While many people can choose the right course of action without the Holy Spirit, I know that *with* the power of the Holy Spirit we can respond with love to an even greater degree and more often.

Even the devout Apostle Paul wrestled with choosing the right thing to do. Listen to his mindset and see if you can relate with him:

> *I'm a mystery to myself, for I want to do what is right, but end up doing what my moral instincts condemn. And if my behavior is not in line with my desire, my conscience still confirms the excellence of the law. And now I realize that it is no longer my true self doing it, but the unwelcome intruder of sin in my humanity. For I know that nothing good lives within the flesh of my fallen humanity. The longings to do what is right are within me, but willpower is not enough to accomplish it. My lofty desires to do what is good are dashed when I do the things I want to avoid. So if my behavior contradicts my desires to do good, I must conclude that it's not my true identity doing it, but the unwelcome intruder of sin hindering me from being who I really am.* (Romans 7:15-20 TPT)

Paul certainly recognized his need for the Holy Spirit to change his life.

4. **Relationship Management** is the result or culmination of using the other three EQ skills. It drives successful relationships through effective communication and conflict management.

EQ takes us right back to Stanley and Frankl.[xxi] It's what we choose to do or not do after ***every statement or response to anyone.*** As believers, we pray we will respond to everyone with love and the fruit of the Spirit: *"love, joy, peace, patience, kindness, goodness, faithfulness, gentleness, and self-control."* (Galations 5:22-23 NIV) When we have a Spirit-led life, we are more attuned to the emotions of others and have the power to respond *humbly with love.*

> *Live in me* [Jesus]. *Make your home in me just as I do in you. In the same way that a branch can't bear grapes by itself but only by being joined to the vine, you can't bear fruit unless you are joined with me.* (John 15:4-5 MSG)

Maturing Those EQ Muscles

Here are eleven ways you can strengthen and mature your EQ muscles.

1. **Become more aware of your feelings and emotions**. The idea is to be able to sense a growing emotion and describe how you are experiencing it. Where does it show up in your physical body? How do you communicate it with your facial expressions and body language? What thoughts go through your mind as you experience a particular emotion? Monitoring your emotions will allow you and the Holy Spirit to best choose a loving, appropriate response or action.

2. **Name your emotion**. The healthiest, highest EQ action you can take is to name your emotions rather than act them out. Acknowledge them to yourself and, then to the others who see them. Generally, as Americans, we lack depth and breadth of emotional vocabulary. We overuse "frustrated" (which is often a euphemism for angry), say we are "happy" or "disappointed" but do not have many more descriptors beyond those. I've included a list of positive and negative emotions in Appendix B. Use this list (or search for "emotion words" on the

Internet for more) to build your emotional language. Saying you're "not great" is not as accurate as "vulnerable", "alone," "pessimistic," or "powerless." Saying you're "fine" is not as accurate as "content," "receptive," or "serene."

3. **Become aware that there are different degrees to what you are feeling; some are stronger than others.** Are you sad or distraught? Happy or elated?

4. **Consider how others may perceive you at different times.** What emotion would others guess they are seeing in you? How can you accurately share what you are feeling with another person?

5. **Check in often with the Holy Spirit.** Ask, "What am I missing?" "What's really going on in me?" "What is really happening in the person with whom I am interacting?"

6. **Watch and listen for non-verbal and emotional information.** Can you name the emotion you see in others? Use the words in Appendix B to name it most accurately.

7. **Talk to others and share your thinking.** Notice the unique perspectives others have. Work hard to

appreciate these as adding more fullness and robustness to your own perspective.

8. **When you are experiencing high negative emotions, take a break**. Go to the Holy Spirit in prayer to help you sort through what triggered the emotion, what thoughts and assumptions are in play, and how you can respond in love. Remember that sometimes the one you need to respond to in love is yourself.

9. **Engage in conversation**. Use the communication skills we've already covered to understand another person's perspective (using other-focused listening and the gift of questions) and best share your own (using your Ladder of Inference, matching body language, and tone of voice).

10. **Ask a trusted friend for feedback.** Use the courage available through the Holy Spirit to ask a trusted co-worker, family member or friend, "How did I come across in that heated discussion?" "What can I do to appear more approachable?" "How appropriately do you think I share my emotions?" "Did you perceive me as gentle and kind?"

11. **Pray for grace** for yourself and those with whom you interact.

IQ can't be changed. It is set in your DNA. But we can raise our EQ, our emotional maturity. That's good news! Hopefully, your self-awareness has already been increased as you've learned skills in the previous chapters in how you listen, ask questions and share your opinion. You are learning tools that can improve your self-expression so you can check in with the Holy Spirit, and then respond with even more *love, joy, peace, patience, kindness, goodness, faithfulness, and gentleness* toward everyone. Intentionally raising your EQ is yet one more way that you can choose to love others well.

> I am convinced that life is 10 percent what happens to me and 90 percent how I react to it.
> *Charles Swindoll*

Self-reflection

1. How do you appear to others? Warm and approachable? Closed and disengaged? What do you want people to see?

2. How well do you recognize specific emotions in your friends, children, co-workers?

3. Do you expect most people to think like you or differently? How surprised are you when someone you know disagrees with you? How do you react to that?

4. Which of the eleven "exercises" above will you turn into a habit?

Additional Reading

- *Emotionally Healthy Spirituality,* Peter Scazzero. 2017, Zondervan
- *Long Way Gone*, Charles Martin. 2016, Thomas Nelson. Martin's fictional characters are so emotionally aware it makes my heart sing!
- *MHS.com*, to purchase an EQ-I 2.0 self-assessment, https://mhs.com/talent-assessments/
- *PositivePsychology.com, 17 Emotional Intelligence Tests and Assessments,* https://positivepsychology.com/emotional-intelligence-tests/

CHAPTER EIGHT

VALUES, VULNERABILITY AND TRUST

Knowing what causes powerful emotions in us and in others is a key to choosing appropriate, loving action. Combine that knowledge with intentional vulnerability and trust, and you have a recipe for increasing the love quotient of your interactions.

Values Influence and Drive Our Emotions

Our core values, which are those principles that we hold most important and dear, are often the source of our strongest emotions. For example, on a catch-up phone call with one of my coworkers, Jack, he casually said to me, "If you get that assignment done on time, we're going to knock the socks off the client." We talked about what we were each doing for the upcoming holiday and how much we enjoy being grandparents.

I hung up with Jack—who was more like a friend to me

than simply a coworker—and I was furious! It took some deep breathing and a conversation with my husband to help me identify why I was so upset: Jack had unintentionally challenged my core value of personal responsibility when he said ***if*** I got the assignment done on time.

So, here's how my furious emotion was connected to one of my highest values, personal responsibility. To me, my word is my bond. I take it seriously. If I say I will do something, I do it or give you plenty of notice if I will need more time. Personal responsibility is one of the chief reasons I fell in love with my husband. He's *so* responsible. It's a characteristic I expressly taught my children. Those are all indicators of how deeply important, how core to my being, personal responsibility is to me.

So, what did I hear when my co-worker innocently stated, "If you get that assignment done on time, we're going to knock the socks off the client"? I heard him question my very character! *Of course*, I would get it done on time! Actually, *he's* the one who always misses deadlines! (I'm using exclamation points so you can "hear" my emotion.) He honestly didn't mean to insult me, but he hit a *core value nerve* in me.

Our perception of whether values are honored or not moderates the intensity of our emotional experience. I will share the outcome of my conversation with Jack in a later chapter.

Unforeseen Reactions

Think of a time when you were in a conversation like the one I had with Jack, where your reaction was immediate and visceral. Sometimes our reactions are disproportionate to another person's intention. We react with *fight* or *flight,* instead of with rational words and actions, as I did with Jack. This overreaction is an indicator that we are **reacting to *something else***—a value dishonored, a hot button, a word or implication that the speaker didn't intend the way we received it.

When you find yourself in a situation like this, my best advice is to ask the Holy Spirit, "*What is really going on in my heart?*" Then listen attentively for his response. Drill down to the why behind your vehement reaction to not only give you valuable insight for future interactions, but to give you more insight into how God has wired you.

When this visceral reaction occurs within you, ask yourself:

- What's the level of intensity?
- Is my natural reaction warranted by the situation? Is it an over-reaction?
- What core value of mine is being dishonored or challenged? What do I need or want that is not being met?
- What can I do to calm the reaction? (Take time out or beat a pillow). Usually, just realizing that it was a hit to our values can lower our emotional response. Having the self-awareness of how important, how core, some things are to us is important to further develop our self-control. In the light cast by the Holy Spirit, we can often discern whether the other person intended to deliver a gut punch, was as surprised as you, or was completely oblivious.

How can you differentiate what needs attention from the visceral reaction you're experiencing? We'll start by identifying your core values so that you are better prepared for intense emotional responses. We'll unpack how to use your communication skills to address the value punch in a later chapter on conflict.

And let's look at it from another's perspective. Have you ever had **your** words and intentions produce an unexpected impact on another person? Instead of a continued rational conversation, you found that the other person *reacted* in an emotional or irrational way? This is an indicator that **they were reacting to *something else***—a hot button, an unrelated issue entangled with the current situation, or *a core value dishonored.*

Identifying your core values

God made us unique: our fingerprints, our DNA, our personality and yes, our core values. What's important to me may not be as important to you. We may have a couple of values in common, but not all. It's not about right and wrong, but different.

Exercise

To help you identify your foundational values, I want to walk you through a brain-storming exercise. I will pose four questions. On a separate piece of paper, write **as many one-word answers to each of the questions as possible**. We want to draw out what might be core to you. If the same word comes up in answer to more than one question, you don't need to write it again. You should aim for 10-20 words on your sheet of paper.

1. Think of a specific friend or your spouse. What traits do you most admire in him or her?

2. Think of one of your children or a favorite child in your life. What do you see in that child that lights you up?

3. What character traits do you think should be taught to everyone?

4. What are your pet peeves? (list the opposite word(s) on the paper or the value that may be in play. For instance, if people arriving late to a meeting or appointment with you are a pet peeve, you might write "punctuality," "respect," "consideration," "courtesy.")

Well done! I suspect your top 3-5 core values are hidden in this list. Read through it slowly. Do any of these words particularly touch your heart? Circle them. Do some come close but do not quite capture what's important to you? Add a synonym. Use this list in conversation with the Holy Spirit to narrow it down to **no more than five words.** It may take an hour or a week. When you have your top three to five values, list them in the left-hand column below.

My Core Values are

1. ________________ ________________________
2. ________________ ________________________
3. ________________ ________________________
4. ________________ ________________________
5. ________________ ________________________

For each of your core values, write a few synonyms or descriptions to the right. This is to help you gain clarity about the word and be able to describe it to others. Your values will be unique to you. One person will have a core value of "Family" and describe it as "my immediate family, spending time at home, being there for my family". Another person with a core value of "Family" might describe it as "duty, comfort, security."

How Values Play Out

My core values are Faith, Authenticity, Personal Responsibility, Communication, and Simplicity and Beauty (yes, I count them as one!). Notice the capital letters. These values are sacred to me and I am sure yours are to you. These five words get to the heart of my identity and are a better name for me than Elle. I think they are closer to what God named me.

When your core values are fully honored in your life by you and others, you will have joy and contentment. Conversely, when you are discontent, unhappy, or disconnected, look at your values. In an instant, you will know which ones need shoring up.

Sometimes, I am the one who dishonors my values. For instance, when I am over-committed, and my life is too complex I will start to recognize an internal discontentment. When I consider my values, I realize the need to say "no" to a few things and restore some Simplicity. Or if I've had a conversation with a friend that didn't go well. I may obsess about it (obsessing can be a values indicator!), realize I didn't communicate well, and plan a time to reconnect and apologize to restore balance to my Communication value.

Occasionally, I have to acknowledge that I am choosing to be in a temporary season of being out of balance with my values. Before my daughter and her family moved 1,200 miles away for a job opportunity, they lived with us for six weeks. I grieved the anticipated loss of half my family while I was delighted that they were in our home. You *can be* sulky and joyful at the same time! Having three grandchildren ages 2, 5 and 8 in our home 24/7 in the depth of winter did not make for "simplicity and beauty". Yet just acknowledging that it was my temporary choice to dishonor that value for a time was enough to calm my soul. Faith, authenticity, personal responsibility and communication filled my heart in the meantime.

Sometimes one or more of your values are dishonored by *others,* as in my conversation with Jack. We'll discuss how to articulate that and how to use your values to improve hard conversations in the chapter, Let Peace Begin with Me.

At other times a core-value clash requires a life change. I was working with a client who had been a capable, and satisfied leader in his organization for years. During a turnover of the Executive Team to which he reported, I noticed he was less and less fulfilled. He looked weary. To me, his new demeanor was an indicator that something was off with his values. As I slowly read his core values to him, tears streamed down his face. "Not *one* of those is valued by the new executive team," he confessed.

What were his options?

1. He could stay and try to change the new team's values. This is rarely successful and can be a steep uphill slog. Imagine someone trying to change *your* values!

2. He could remain and ignore his emotions. This would eventually show up as physical and/or emotional distress.

3. He could leave.

How long did it take for him to choose an option? Before I could even outline them for him, he blew his nose and said, "I have to get a different job."

> It's not hard to make decisions when you know what your values are.
>
> *Roy Disney, Former Vice Chairman, Walt Disney Company*

You will suffer if you have *daily* value conflicts. My husband went through a similar work challenge. He tried option #1, above, for months. He was in a senior leadership position, so he thought he could influence the organization's values to align more with his. But values are deeply held. The day he walked away, he arrived home a renewed man, taller, lighter and truly content. He didn't have another job waiting for him but being true to his values more than made up for it. He could hold his head high and sense a fuller heart; he felt right with himself and with God.

Identifying others' core values

To know and honor the values of other's is a sign of high emotional intelligence, respect and love. Just as you want others to honor your values, you need to do the same for them. Jesus taught us this aspect of loving others:

> *Ask yourself what you want people to do for you; then grab the initiative and do it for them*! (Luke 6:31 MSG)

When you understand what is profoundly important to the people in your life, you can honor their values through your actions and words. How do you learn other people's core values?

Ask - Engage people with good questions and then listen carefully to their answers. Here are some examples:

- "What characteristics do you look for in a best friend?"
- When you choose a new hire, what character traits are important criteria for you?"
- What do you want to be sure to instill in your children?"
- What are your pet peeves with people?" (the opposite is a clue to their core values)

Observe - People generally live in a way that is in harmony with their core values. Watch for clues as to what is important in a person's life. You might not get the exact right word, but you can confirm it with the individual. For example, this is how you could identify and confirm my core values.

- If you visited my home, you would see that I decorate it in neutrals and have few extraneous items. I rarely wear prints on my clothing. I have carefully chosen pieces of art. "Elle, it seems like Simplicity and Aesthetics are important to you." "Yes! I call it Simplicity and Beauty. I see beauty in simplicity. I even see beauty in a highly functional, high-trust team."

- I wear Christian jewelry; I have a cross prominently displayed in my home and my Bibles are readily visible there. "Elle, your faith seems central to who you are." "Yes! Faith is one of my core values."

- I am fanatical about arriving early for appointments. "Elle, I think you value punctuality." "I'd call it Personal Responsibility, but you're right! Thanks for noticing!"

- I passionately teach about healthy communication and want to talk out any perceived disagreements. "Elle, is good communication pretty important to you?"

Listen - What words do people use to describe what lights them up or brings them down? If you were with me, you would hear that:

- I frequently use the words "responsibility" and "accountability"—and when I do, there's passion in my tone of voice.

- I openly share my faith, and what God is doing in my life.

- I use "authenticity" as a high compliment.

As you discover a person's values, write them down. I put them in the person's contact information under "Notes" on my phone. It's a demonstration of love to be interested in learning their values and to acknowledge them when you see them. "Gideon, when you gave that presentation yesterday, you really honored your value of conciseness." It also shows "*kindness, and goodness*" when you honor someone's core values in your interactions with him.

We gravitate toward people who share at least some of our values. When you consider your closest friends and co-workers, you will see your core values overlap with theirs. Yet Jesus taught us to *"Love your enemies, do good to those who hate you*" (Luke 6:27 NIV). As I have discussed above, it is challenging to daily work with someone whose values are "enemies," or opposite to yours.

While we may not befriend or marry someone who has different values than ours, we are called to show kindness and goodness to everyone. We'll look at this in more depth in the chapter, Love Who?! You are called to **love everyone**, but you do not have to **accept their values as yours.** As a pro-lifer who passionately embraces this issue as a part of my core value of Faith, I have a "values' conflict" with someone who values the right to take innocent, pre-born life. But I will be obediently *compassionate, kind, humble, gentle and patient* with them. *I will bear with them and forgive them.* (Colossians 3:10 NIV)

They are called core values for a reason. They're our North Star, a guide in the dark, planted by God to have us be true to the unique person he created. Live, lead, and love by your core values.

Vulnerability

Self-expression is choosing what we will do and what actions we will or will not take in response to what we see in others and ourselves. As I've said, it's synonymous with self-control. Self-expression is our "Respond-ability Superpower" and has many forms—from a subtle shift of the eyes to a loud shout.

Vulnerability is one of many responses we can choose that will specifically enhance our relationships. To be vulnerable is the "humble" in *serve one another humbly in love* (Galatians 5:13-14 NIV). Instead of only putting forth a perfect version of me, I choose to let you see my shortcomings and flaws as well. Being vulnerable is about sharing more of ourselves than we might naturally, in order to go deeper in our relationships. It is a conscious choice to share more of me with you—my heart and thoughts, weaknesses, and imperfections. When I choose this path, I also hope to hear more of your heart and thoughts and therefore to build greater understanding and compassion between us.

Appropriately revealing yourself to build trust and connection is key to deepening relationships. But I want to make an important distinction. It is not about over-sharing or interrupting or telling your own story too soon, as in self-focused listening. The stories I tell about myself in this book are an example of vulnerability. I have shared some of my successes, but I have also let you see my flaws and limitations, so you see that I am a person with good stuff, hard stuff and awful stuff—just like you.

Two of the foremost desires of humans are to be known and to be loved. Our all-sufficient God supplies these perfectly and completely; we are fully known and unconditionally loved by him. But to be deeply known and loved by other humans is much harder to come by, and some of that is our own doing. We are constantly choosing how much we can share about ourselves—be known—and still be loved. In every conversation we decide the level of vulnerability we will display. For example, I choose not to tell the person I just met on the Pickleball court about my recent visit to the doctor. But I will easily share it with a trusted friend who I can count on for empathy and confidentiality.

When we are getting to know each other in a new group, we often share something about our backgrounds. Some may choose to share more general information, such as the names and ages of their children. Others might choose to be more vulnerable and talk about one of their most tender, frightening, or sad times. It's an issue of trust. We judge how "safe" or trustworthy the audience is and what level of risk we want to take.

Some of us trust easily and will share extensively. Others are slower to reveal themselves. Our life experiences and personalities are part of the equation in how quickly and easily we trust.

Shame and Vulnerability

We are less likely to share with others those things of which we are ashamed. We assume we will be judged poorly, shut out, and *not loved*, if we share our faults and imperfections. Satan repeats that assumption to make us believe it is accurate. Through her extensive research, well-known vulnerability researcher and author, Brené

Brown, PhD, MSW, found that, "Shame derives its power from being unspeakable."[xxii] This is one of Satan's best techniques to keep us isolated from other's. The lie he whispers is that people will only love us if we keep our shameful behavior hidden inside us. Then he uses that shamefulness to expand our sense of unworthiness—that we are not worthy of being loved or even worse, that we are unlovable.

Vulnerability fights that lie. If you talk about the baby you gave up for adoption at 16, you take shame's power and expose it to God's light, depriving Satan of his power. And you make it safer for your listener to share something that she has been hiding and carrying. You allow God's light in and shrink the darkness in her.

The more worthy we feel and the more we embrace *God's* unconditional love for us, the more we'll take a risk and allow people to really see us.

The opposite of vulnerability is to approach the world wearing a mask—a mask of what you *think* others want to see. **You choose not to be fully seen**. The problem with a mask is that you don't see me, and I do not see you. Neither of us will be known. Conversely, when we choose to be appropriately vulnerable and lower our masks, we draw people to a deeper relationship with us.

When I take down my mask of perfection to let you see the real me, I communicate that I trust you and I create a safe place for you to be yourself.

If I choose *not* to share what I expect of you and our relationship—I keep it hidden behind a mask—how can you possibly meet my expectations even if you wanted to? Unvoiced expectations lead to *unmet* expectations. Revealing what I'd like to see happen, what my values are and what I expect from people allows others to meet those expectations. To withhold what we expect and then rebuke others when they do not meet our unspoken expectations is an unhealthy game we play. Ask the Holy Spirit to daylight when you have done this so that you can choose to correct it.

Vulnerability, Courage and Love

What does vulnerability have to do with loving others? Brown succinctly addresses this in her June 2010, TED Talk, *The Power of Vulnerability,*[xxiii] which has been viewed over 51 million times. She has discovered that vulnerability is the very definition of courage and **the key to connection.** By being vulnerable, you "go first" in taking a risk with the other person. You make it safe for them to choose to share more since you've "exposed" yourself to them. As a facilitator I've witnessed that, in a group, no one will be more vulnerable than the "norm" that is established by the first people who speak. If someone starts with "the day my car broke down," it will take much more courage for someone to share "My spouse just left me."

James the brother of Jesus, taught us this practice:

> *Therefore, confess your sins* [shame] *to each other and pray for each other* **so that** *you may be healed.* (James 5:16 NIV addition mine)

Ask the Holy Spirit to help you determine appropriate vulnerability—how much to share and what to withhold. Allow him to push you out of your comfort zone, to deepen relationships in your life.

> The irony is that we attempt to disown our difficult stories to appear more whole or more acceptable but our wholeness – even our wholeheartedness – actually depends on the integration of all our experiences, including the falls. *Brené Brown PhD, MSW*

Inviting Vulnerability from Others

You can invite *others* to be more vulnerable by asking meaningful questions as in the chapter on The Gift of Asking. One of our pastors is a master at this. We had spoken to him two times over lunch about how we wanted to be involved in our church, and then we asked him and his wife to have dinner at our home. We didn't know each other well. Yet look at the level of questions he asked:

> "How do you stay married as two, Type A personalities?"
>
> "Are you best friends?"

It was even shocking to me as a transparent extrovert! Yet his questions let me know he'd been hyper-focused in his listening (we didn't *say* we were type A's) and wanted to *know us* on a deeper level. His tone of voice told me he would accept me no matter how I answered and that he'd answer the same questions if we asked.

In her TED Talk and because of her research, Brown encourages us to grow our vulnerability quotient by "Let[ting] yourself be *seen*. Love with your whole heart. Practice gratitude and joy. Believe you are enough."[xxiv]

Sounds like something Jesus would have advised.

Self-reflection

1. How will you use the knowledge of your core values?

2. Where are you on the trust continuum? Do you trust easily, or does it take a long time for people to earn your trust?

3. What is your prayer regarding trust and vulnerability with others and with God?

Exercise

Choose a person you'd like to know more deeply; a friendship you want to grow. Use a couple of the suggestions from the Core Values Exercise to uncover what's really important to him/her. Use hyper-focused listening to seek to more fully understand that person.

Additional Reading

- *Daring Greatly,* Brené Brown Ph.D. 2012 Avery
- *The Gifts of Imperfection: Let Go of Who You Think You're Supposed to Be and Embrace Who You Are*, Brené Brown Ph.D. 2010, Hazelden Publishing
- *Safe People: How to Find Relationships that are Good for You and Avoid Those That Aren't*, Henry Cloud and John Townsend. 2016, Zondervan
- *The Seven Longings of the Human Heart*, Mike Bickle with Deborah Hiebert. 2006, Forerunner Books, International House of Prayer–Kansas City

CHAPTER NINE

ATTITUDE AND AVAILABILITY

Love requires that we selflessly give our time, talent, money and/or attitude to others. These are precious to us, which is why we exhibit love when we give them away. However, the skills I have introduced to you, or reminded you of, **require no money and little additional time**. It's about using our time with others more wisely, with a selfless attitude, and weaving new habits of love into our everyday lives.

Generosity of Attitude

Generosity in attitude is about shifting our focus from ourselves to others more often and more intentionally. We breathe a spirit of generosity into our relationships when we choose to react from a different heart place than we might in our self-interested, natural way. Again, we can't do this without taking that all-important pause to listen to the Holy Spirit. *Then* we can respond with an attitude of *compassion, kindness, humility, gentleness and patience, serving humbly with love.*

To achieve generosity in our attitude, we need the Holy Spirit to help us overcome a sizeable negative propensity. This propensity has been around since Adam and Eve, and it's called The Fundamental Attribution Error (FAE).[xxv] We have a tendency to assume that other people's actions are entirely defined by their personal characteristics and not by situational or external factors. In contrast, we think that *our* behavior is because of situational factors. Very simply, at a fundamental level, we naturally attribute more grace to ourselves than others. Let me illustrate.

I was driving down a two-lane road and up ahead I saw a blinking arrow pointing left, indicating a narrowing down to one lane. I am such a good, law-abiding citizen I merged to the left as soon as possible. Meanwhile, cars flew by me on the right in an attempt to get to the front of the line. *They're selfish,* flashed through my mind. *They think they're more important than me.* I was irritated and tried to ease to the right a bit to block them. Am I alone? Have you been there?

Then, on a different day, I was driving along thinking of what we would have for dinner and whether I needed to stop at the store. Suddenly, I had to merge left. I had missed the warning sign a half-mile back! I was terribly embarrassed. I gave the little thank-you wave to the person who let me in, and said, "I'm sorry!" out loud in the car. It was just a mistake. I wasn't paying attention. I didn't do it on purpose!

Do you hear the difference in these two examples? When I err, I attribute it to extenuating circumstances and give myself a bucket load of grace. When others err, I immediately assume they are not pleasant people and have selfish motives. This happens ALL THE TIME. Another name for the FAE is SIN. So, when we want to use our Respond-ability Superpower, we must fight a built-in instinct to react as if the other party has malicious intent *unless* we take advantage of that God-given gap between stimulus and response to listen to the Holy Spirit's guidance.

> *For by the grace given me I say to every one of you: Do not think of yourself more highly than you ought, but rather think of yourself with sober judgment, in accordance with the faith God has distributed to each of you.* (Romans 12:3 NIV)

> Everything in my own immediate experience supports my deep belief that I am the absolute center of the universe; the realist, most vivid and important person in existence. We rarely think about this sort of natural, basic self-centeredness because it's so socially repulsive. But it's pretty much the same for all of us. It is our default setting, hard-wired into our boards at birth.
>
> *David Foster Wallace*

By Contrast

Jesus didn't have an FAE or SIN. Look at how he handled the ultimate injustice:

> *When they came to the place called The Skull, they crucified Him there, along with the criminals, one on His right and the other on His left. Jesus said* [as the blood trickled down from under his crown of thorns, from the spikes hammered into his wrists and ankles and his flogged, flayed back], ***"Father, forgive them, for they do not know what they are doing."*** *And they divided up his clothes by casting' lots.* (Luke 23: 33-34 NIV emphasis mine)

In my flesh, love and forgiveness is not the first reaction I have to the person who cuts me off, the friend who betrays me, the teacher who is harsh, or the drunk driver who kills a child. Are we able to adopt the attitude of, *"Father, forgive them, for they do not know what they are doing?"* We are, but only with the prompting and power of the Holy Spirit.

Catching Ourselves

We recently changed health insurance providers and received the first invoice which clearly stated, "Visit [the website] and click 'Pay Your Premium.'" *That will be so easy,* I happily thought! Thirty minutes later having searched high and low on the website for such a button, having called the phone number offered, having "spoken" to the computerized agent, and having been transferred to three different "customer service representatives," my blood was boiling.

The final customer service rep, Wayne, explained that I had to go to a completely *different* website **than the one listed on the invoice**. It, too, was not "customer-friendly," but it did at least have a "Pay Your Premium" button. Once you hit that "button" on each of no less than three pages, you could actually pay your premium. This process had no resemblance at all to the deceptive instructions on the invoice in front of me. My core values of Responsibility and Simplicity had been flung on the ground and repeatedly stomped into the dirt. I was mad.

I had no thought to check with the Spirit as I unloaded on my husband about how irresponsible the company was to send out an invoice with the wrong information on it. He kindly and gently reminded me, "Elle, you sent out an invoice for your work last week that contained errors. They returned it to you to correct." Oh yeah.

There it was! Sin in the form of the Fundamental Attribution Error. I had given myself loads of grace and explained my mistake with situational factors. Yet, I attacked the very character of the insurance company with no grace for their error. If Jesus could say, "*Father, forgive them, for they do not know what they are doing?*" after he was *nailed to a cross*, I should be able to say it after a slight from my insurance company. Humility. I need more humility as Paul commanded:

> *With tender humility and quiet patience, always demonstrate gentleness and generous love toward one another, especially toward those who may try your patience.* (Ephesians 4:2 TPT)

I Don't Want To

We have a choice. We can have a self*less* attitude or a self*ish* attitude. What does love require? Christ told us to *obey* his teaching and commands. Dictionary.com defines "obey" as to "comply with or follow commands, restrictions, wishes or instructions; to submit or conform in action."

Some days, some moments, my attitude is far from wanting to obey the command *Serve one another humbly in love* (Gal 5:13-14 NIV). I justify that because of my current circumstances, I am ***incapable*** of obeying. That's when I pray to the Spirit with a grudge in my voice, "What does love require?" and then I *comply* like an ungrateful servant. If I only used the tools in this book when I *felt* like it, I would be a rebellious servant indeed.

> *May the God who gives endurance and encouragement give* ***you the attitude of mind toward each other*** *that Christ Jesus had, SO THAT with one mind and one voice you may* ***glorify the God and Father of our Lord Jesus Christ*** (Romans 15:5-6 NIV emphasis mine)

There's an enormous gap between Jesus and us. It will be a lifelong journey to behave more like him—to be sanctified. He knows it. He rejoices with each step we take toward him.

The only accurate way to understand ourselves is by what God is and by what he does for us, not by what we are and what we do for him. (Romans 12:3b MSG)

The Learning Curve

Throughout this book, I have asked you to try on new behaviors to respond more lovingly to others. Some of them you already do very well; they are second nature and you are not even aware of doing them. Others are brand new and when you "try them on" they don't seem to fit your style or are constrictive, thus eroding your confidence. There's a logical explanation for this.

As we learn a new skill or try on a new behavior, we move through four stages.[xxvi]

1. Unconscious Incompetence
2. Conscious Incompetence
3. Conscious Competence
4. Unconscious Competence

Let's use learning to drive a car to illustrate these stages. When you passed your Learner's Permit test you couldn't wait to get behind the wheel of the family car. You had been a passenger your entire life and watched Mom and Dad drive you everywhere. This is going to be so easy!

You were more than ready to drive home from the Department of Motor Vehicles. That's **Unconscious Incompetence**; you had all the confidence of youth, but you had no idea what this new skill would take.

Then you sat behind the wheel and used the accelerator and brake for the first time. Zoom! Slam! *That's not what I thought it would be like* might have crossed your mind. Your courageous Mom had wisely taken you to an empty parking lot and you clumsily made your way around it. You realized in an instant that this was going to be harder than you expected. You might even have thought, *"I'll NEVER get this right.* Or, *I never want to drive on the Interstate!* That's **Conscious Incompetence**. You were suddenly fully aware of how bad you were at this new skill.

After driving with a parent at your side for several weeks, you were a bit more relaxed and much smoother when you sped up and slowed down. But you were using *every brain cell to do it*. It took intentionality, a quiet parent and intense concentration to get it right. That is **Conscious Competence**. You were a competent driver, but you needed to be fully engaged and conscious of what you were doing.

Then you finally reached the glorious stage of **Unconscious Competence.** You could drive solo while singing along to your favorite song on the radio, and munching on fries. You "magically" arrived at your destination and couldn't remember how you got there.

As adults, we want Unconscious Competence immediately after we are introduced to a new skill. We are impatient and embarrassed if we do not get it right (perfect) the first time we try it. In order to have the **attitude of Christ**, you will need to expect, and choose to be comfortable with each stage. It's OK to "fall down" or be clumsy when you first try to add non-judgmental questions to your conversations or to be more vulnerable. You may think, *I'll never get this right,* and you might be tempted to decide, *There's no point in trying.*

What would happen if a baby came to that conclusion when she learned to walk? As you would with a child, be patient with yourself as you put on these new skills. It takes humility to serve others in love.

> The secret of life is to fall seven times and to get up eight times. *Paul Coelho*

Availability—Giving of Your Time

In his book, *Margin: Restoring Emotional, Physical, Financial, and Time Reserves to Overloaded Lives,*[xxvii] Dr. Richard Swenson makes the case that we've filled up our lives so much that we do not have any "margin" or availability for the unplanned. If there's no margin in our lives, we can't be available to serve others when they really need it.

As I tumbled into bed one night, exhausted, during a season of too many commitments, I realized I had done nothing well that day. I let everyone down, giving quality time to nothing and no one. It is not where I wanted to be. The non-profit organizations to which I was giving my time were worthy causes, but I had no quality time available for my children, husband or friends.

After soaking up Dr. Swenson's wisdom, I determined to pare down my scheduled activities so that I could be readily available for the important relationships in my life. If a friend called to say her husband had lung cancer, I wanted to run to her in short order and have time to sit and listen with hyper-focus. When my husband came home after a tough day at the office, I yearned to put aside dinner prep and give him my undivided attention. I became much more skilled in recognizing when I had to say, "no," so that I could say, "yes," to what really mattered—investing in the people God entrusted to me.

While the practices in this book do not take much more time, you do need room or margin in your life to do them. When you are over-booked and over-committed, you lose the capacity to choose to *serve one another humbly in love*. You won't have the time or the mental and emotional capacity.

Here are God's promises to you as you adopt an attitude like the child of the king you are and become aware of, and available for, the nudges of the Spirit.

> *Good friend don't forget all I've taught you;* ***take to heart my commands****. They'll help you live a long, long time,* ***a long life lived full and well****. Don't lose your grip on Love and Loyalty. Tie them around your neck; carve their initials on your heart.* [sounds like God's core values] ***Earn a reputation for living well in God's eyes and the eyes of the people.*** *Trust God from the bottom of your heart; don't try to figure out everything on your own.* ***Listen for God's voice in everything you do, everywhere you go;*** *he's the one who will keep you on track. Don't assume that you know it all. Run to God! Run from evil! Your body will glow with health,* ***your very bones will vibrate with life****!* (Proverbs 3:1-8 MSG)

> What if we stopped celebrating being busy as a measurement of importance? What if instead we celebrated how much time we had spent listening, pondering, meditating, and enjoying time with the most important people in our lives?
>
> *Greg McKeown*

Self-reflection

1. To whom do you easily give grace? In what situations, or with whom, do you too easily assume evil or poor intent?

2. Ask God where he wants you to adjust your attitude.

3. On a scale of 1 to 10, 10 being so over-committed that you can't see straight, how much margin do you have in your life? Ask the Holy Spirit where you should pare back to be more available for his priorities.

Additional Reading

- *Boundaries, When to Say Yes, How to Say No to Take Control of Your Life*, Henry Cloud and John Townsend. 2017, Zondervan.
- *Margin: Restoring Emotional, Physical, Financial, and Time Reserves to Overloaded Lives*, Richard Swenson, M.D. 2004, NavPress

CHAPTER TEN

AUTHENTIC EMPATHY

Rejoice with those who rejoice [sharing others' joy]; mourn with those who mourn [sharing others' grief]. (Romans 12:15 AMP)

Therefore, as God's chosen people, holy and dearly loved, clothe yourselves with compassion, kindness, humility, gentleness and patience. (Colossians 3:10a NIV)

When someone has been compassionate, gentle, and kind to me, I know it—I feel it deep in my heart. Expressing it to someone else is harder for me. I've observed that *generally*, we 21st Century humans are not very skilled at quality empathy—the ability to experience and express the emotions, thoughts, and attitudes of another.

Empathy is a conscious choice, enhanced by the wisdom of the Holy Spirit, to see and feel what another person is experiencing. It is Social Awareness at its best. Empathy allows us to do what Paul encourages in the verse from Romans above—to be happy with those who are happy and sad with those who are sad. When emotion is apparent in the person in front of us—a stranger or a friend—too often our instinct is to avoid it or go straight to trying to solve the person's problem. Or, worse, steamroll over those emotions and tell our own story of happiness or woe in a sad display of self-focused listening.

Nursing scholar, Theresa Wiseman[xxviii] outlines the four attributes of empathy that Brené Brown PhD, MSW references in her extensive research on the subject.

1. Perspective taking
2. Staying out of judgment
3. Recognizing emotion in others
4. Communicating it

1. Perspective taking.

In the previous chapter, Words and Impressions, we addressed the Ladder of Inference that depicts how you view the world. Empathy requires us to quiet or silence our own "ladder," or viewpoint, in order to picture the other person's perspective. In the situation the person finds herself, what data has she selected to focus on? What meaning has she ascribed to what she has seen and heard? What conclusions has she come to?

I have a friend who heard a disheartening, long-term health diagnosis from his doctor. I have never received such challenging health news. When he called to share the news with me, I was tempted to say, "*I can't imagine what you're going through.*" But I *can* choose to *try* to see the circumstance through his eyes. I can choose empathy.

As we spoke, I asked him questions to help me better understand all that he was going through. "Where is your focus?" "What scares you the most?" "What emotions are forefront?" "What has surprised you?"

You might think *that's so intrusive*! *That's way too personal.* It is certainly different from what our culture teaches. We want to gloss over the hard stuff, give a hug, say we'll pray for the person and move on. It takes courage and hyper-focused listening to do this well—to not rush through the conversation but to give **the gift of a safe place to talk.** I invited him to share his thoughts and experiences. I opened the door for him to articulate the fears and emotions with which he was wrestling.

Too often our first question is, "What can I do to help?"

We so desperately want to do something, to take action, anything to rescue our friend from his thoughts and emotions. But there are two reasons to not lead with this: 1) he needs to process through the maelstrom of thoughts and emotions in his head before he can answer such a practical question, and 2) you can't fix what he needs fixed.

I can't cure my friend. Do I know a specialist in his area of diagnosis? Maybe. But this isn't the time. When his head and heart are a blur, asking such tactical, "head" questions like how I can help, is not the most loving move. Choose to sit and wait with him in his grief and confusion. Allow him to process. Check in with the Spirit before you switch to the practical. He will feel infinitely more known and loved.

God is such a good and patient teacher for me. A close friend of mine has a daughter who is trying to compete with the Prodigal Son in rebelliousness. As I was writing this very chapter, I felt a strong desire to call her and suggest she be more empathetic with her daughter. So I did. What was I thinking?! My *friend* needed empathy, not a solution that I made up in my head! For almost a decade, she and her husband have done their best; using every resource imaginable to help their daughter. Why did I think I should just pick up the phone and give her useful advice?? Lesson learned … again and again. I could have served my friend so much better that day if I had taken the first moments of our call to listen to her emotions and pain.

2. Staying out of judgment.

Along with seeing a situation from another's perspective, true empathy calls for us to avoid judgment. As Brené Brown, PhD, MSW notes, "This is hard. Especially for those of us who enjoy it so much!" Ouch!

Back to my friend with the health issue. Did his lifestyle contribute to his diagnosis? Yes. Would it contribute to him feeling loved if I mention it? No. Is that already a part of his "ladder" or perspective? Of course. **When people experience powerful emotions, they need empathy, not judgment.** Unfortunately, I expect my girlfriend felt judged as I explained how she could be more empathetic to her daughter.

I will exaggerate to reinforce the concept. If my child fell out of a tree and the radius bone in her arm was sticking out of her skin, is it loving to ask, "What made you climb the tree?!" Or to give advice: "Next time try not to fall." Of course not! She wants to, needs to, hear that I am experiencing her pain with her. "Honey, where does it hurt the most?"

If my son gets a dreadful grade on a school paper, opening with, "I told you to turn the TV off and study more," will not make him feel loved. A better response to that stimulus would be, "You must be disappointed, crushed," and then move to hyper-focused listening. After you hear his emotions adequately—or better yet, the next morning—you might gently ask, "What would you like to do differently when your next paper is due?" It won't hurt to delay a solution or "lesson." To wait in order to provide adequate empathy will make the person feel understood and loved despite their mistake.

3. Recognizing emotion in others.

Social awareness includes accurately discerning emotions in others and is one element of emotional intelligence we discussed in More EQ, Please. If I am with a friend who is hurting, I will probably see evidence of emotion on her face and in the way she holds herself. If I am on the phone, I might hear it in her tone of voice. If I get the news via email or text, I can only try to *imagine* the emotions. The first act of love when I see that text is to choose to pick up the phone to let her know I want to understand her crisis and the depth of her emotion. I can pull out the list of emotions in Appendix B to put a name to those I imagine she is experiencing. I want to let my friend know I "hear" them.

For example, "Kelsey, [who just learned she didn't get the promotion for which she thought she was the top candidate] I'm thinking you're discouraged, disillusioned, angry…" or "What are some emotions churning in you?"

As a reminder, steer clear of "How does that make you feel?" No matter how much you monitor your tone of voice, it can easily be perceived as trite.

4. Communicating it.

This is the part that takes vulnerability and courage. In my examples above I risked being wrong in my guess of the person's emotions, or of offending her. But I communicated that I was *trying* to hear them correctly. People will quickly respond to help you in your endeavor to understand. "I'm not disappointed, I am furious!" Or, "I am not discouraged. I'm really mad at myself." It's OK to get it wrong when your genuine intent is to appreciate the situation and empathize.

How to Communicate Empathy

When we are in pain, we want to be heard and understood. It's a gift of love to allow someone a safe place to "vent" their emotion and give him or her the gift of hyper-focused listening. You will hear a rewarding, "Thank you so much for listening."

Here are some examples of how to invite a person to share their inner struggle with you:

- "Tell me more."
- "How is [the issue] affecting you? Your work? Home life?" Seek first to understand.
- "I wonder if you're feeling (name several emotions)."
- "What is the greatest hardship right now?" "Greatest joy?"
- "Where is it showing up in your body?" When I've asked this, I've heard, "It's a gut punch." "My heart is broken." "My jaw is clenched from the stress." Your goal is to learn more and more about what the person is experiencing and communicate that you care enough to ask.
- Listen for the words they are using to describe their situation and ask them to

expand on them. "You said you feel powerless. Tell me more." Or maybe your friend tells you about something he is excited about rather than something he is struggling with. You could reply, "You said you're enthusiastic. What excites you most?"

Remember to avoid asking "Why?" as described in the chapter on questions.

Another phrase to avoid is "at least," as in:

- "My marriage is falling apart." "At least you have your wonderful children!"
- "I didn't get the (new) job." "At least you have a job!"
- "My mom died." "(At least) she had a long life!"

Better alternatives are:

- "My marriage is falling apart." "Tell me what's going on."
- "I didn't get the (new) job." "That's so disappointing! What emotions are running through you?"

- "My mom died." "What an immense hole you must have in your heart. What special memories are surfacing? What about her do you already miss?"

Self-focused listening is the *opposite* of empathy. I recently saw an excellent example of self-focused listening and empathy in my Nextdoor phone app.

New Entry: Just lost a brand new (sic) puppy.

Response: So sorry, I had my 5 month old (sic) Siamese kitten picked up by a bird probably a owl (sic) since it was early evening when she got out. She followed the older cat out through the cat door. I saw the little paw prints come to a dead stop in the snow. She was only 4 pounds and I'm still broken-hearted after almost a month.

(A different) Response: Any news on your precious puppy?

> **Reply**: No thanks trying to think positive
>
> **Reply**: Will be praying he's warm & safe tonight. I'm so sorry you and your family are having to go through the night not knowing

Yes, we can choose to offer empathy—or not—in texts, emails and social media. Which neighbor showed empathy in her response? Which neighbor chose self-focused listening? Self-focused listening is especially ugly and selfish when used in response to a person who is suffering.

When a person has had the courage to be vulnerable and share a part of himself, take the time to look at his heart with the help of the Spirit:

1. Take on his perspective
2. Stay out of judgment
3. Recognize his emotions
4. Acknowledge that you see those emotions (communicate)

> *The Lord does not look at the things people look at. People look at the outward appearance, but the Lord looks at the heart.* (1 Samuel 16:7 NIV)

Feelings *then* Facts *then* Solutions

When I experience strong emotions, I literally can't hear the facts of the situation or a solution until you prove to me that you have "heard" my emotions. Am I alone in this? All of us need to process our emotions and have them recognized before we can open our ears to logic.

When my son was five years old, he fell and skinned his knee while running on the sidewalk at a state park. He was hysterical. Embarrassingly hysterical. I mean screaming, crying, and moaning. It appeared to be a relatively minor scrape, but I am sure bystanders thought we had cut off his foot. In my calmest I-don't-want-to-be-reported-to-social-services voice, I kept telling him we would clean it up and get a Band-Aid. I offered him facts and solutions. He cried even louder.

I propelled him toward the Visitors' Center, where I was sure there would be a first-aid kit. He stumbled dramatically, sat down, and grabbed his knee, acting like he had severed an artery. I never once thought to stop, sit down *with him,* and just empathize with his pain. People—children and grownups alike—**will act out their emotions until they are acknowledged,** and no amount of logical facts and solutions will break through.

I experienced this first-hand one December 21st. I was out of town, nearly finished with a training event in Dallas, and eager to get home and wrap presents to prepare for Christmas. At lunch my travel agent called to say, "Don't worry. I have you on a flight home on December 27th." I knew she must have the wrong client.

As a mother of two high-school kids, I had been very careful to plan to be home in plenty of time for Christmas. "Oh, no. I fly home tonight," I confidently corrected her.

"Have you been watching the news?" she queried. "There is a huge snowstorm in Denver. Hundreds of flights are cancelled, and because it's Christmas, there are no seats on any flights into Denver until December 27th." This news felt devastating, but I tried to stay calm. I had four more hours in front of a group before I could even think about alternative solutions. I know I was physically shaking from trying to contain the emotions that flooded my system as I walked back to the training room.

At the end of class, my husband called to say cheerfully, "I've solved the problem! I have you booked on a Greyhound bus and you'll get home in 18 hours." Again, I'm an adult and I teach other adults about interpersonal relationship skills so you would think I would just instinctively know that I needed to process my emotions. But I was struggling. I focused on maintaining my cool and tried to think logically, but I was fighting to do so. I made my way to the bus station—looking *way* overdressed in my pencil-skirt suit and leather briefcase—and stood in line to pick up my ticket from

Will Call.

I showed the clerk my electronic confirmation, and he stated the facts plainly, "You can't get on the bus. No one going to Denver can get on the bus". Just the facts. Panic and anger rose in me. "Can I go to Amarillo?" I figured I could rent a car there and drive the rest of the way. "No. You can't get on the bus." Tears flowed freely down my face. I could not maintain my professional demeanor a moment longer. I was acting out all the emotional baggage I had held back since lunchtime. Then he hit me with his solution, "It's OK," he declared, "I'll give you a full refund."

OK?? It's not OK!! He had gone straight to his idea for a solution while denying what was right in front of him: a blubbering, weeping, emotional woman begging him to reconsider. Finally, a man behind me in line said, "Hey, she's upset. She just wants to be with her family for Christmas!" He heard me, saw me, understood. A total stranger gave me what love required. But that's not the end of the story.

How did I get home? A dear friend who lived in the area offered her solution: I could spend Christmas with her family! My heart yearned for home, so she retrieved me from the bus station and took me to the rental car desk at the airport. I got the last car in the lot. Faced with an 18-hour drive alone in the dark, I sniveled and sobbed as I signed the papers at the rental desk. The clerk was completely ignoring my obvious distress. Then my BFF whispered firmly in my ear, "Stop. Crying." She squeezed my bicep to be sure she had made her point. "They won't rent you this car if they think you're crazy!" (You're right. I'm not proud of this episode.)

Somehow, I made it two hours north in my rental car, alternatively bawling and whimpering. Both my friend and my husband had stepped in with solutions, but I still didn't feel *understood.* Then my phone died.

How could I get home without my lifeline to my family? It was as pitch dark as it can only be in rural Texas. There was nothing as far as I could see. Suddenly, an IHOP® appeared ahead like Oz itself! I pulled in, staggered to the cash register and gave a short-hand version of my plight to the server—working hard to stop the tears—and asked if I could plug in my phone somewhere. *No one* had acknowledged my emotions of anguish and helplessness, so I was still *acting out.* I knew I probably looked like a lunatic, but I didn't care. The server quickly took my phone and promised she would plug it in as she guided me to one of the many empty booths. Interestingly, she didn't say, "I'm so sorry." More on that below.

What did this stranger do next? She asked if she could sit down at my table and she asked to hear the entire story. She didn't ask me to look at the menu while I was so emotional. She just listened as I poured out my no-good-very-bad day. It was 9:00 p.m. and I told her I'd been up since 5:00 a.m., but that I intended to drive the next 16 hours straight through since I was desperate to get home. She listened attentively, told me what a ghastly situation I was in, and then took my order.

When she brought my food, she again asked to join me. She told me she had been a 911 Operator and knew the dangerous places along my route. *Without my telling her,* she had sensed my fear of the journey with her hyper-focused listening. She handed me a piece of paper with the "safe" rest areas and those I was to avoid, gave me her parents' address and phone number in Amarillo and explained they would be happy to have me stop and sleep there. She really did!

I was speechless. This kind stranger hadn't asked, "How can I help you?" I couldn't have possibly answered intelligently. But she had **listened at such a depth that she inferred what would be of use to me.** I was already better, and my heart pounded less by the time we finished talking. Gone were the tears. When I asked for the check, she told me the dinner was on her and handed me a giant cup of hot coffee for the road. You might think she was a kind stranger who scored an A+ in empathy, but I am pretty sure she was an angel sent by God.

We Can Do Better than "I'm Sorry"

When we hear that something tragic has befallen a co-worker, friend, family member, or stranger, our standard default response is, "I'm so sorry." It's what automatically comes out when we do not ask ourselves, "What does love require?" Mind you, saying this won't hurt anyone, but followers of Christ can do better.

First, what are we sorry for? We didn't cause the pain. Maybe we mean, "I'm sorry I can't fix it." They know that. It's hollow. Often, we mean, "I feel sadness because of what happened." Again, we are stating the obvious, and it's trite.

A better response is to go to our empathy questions and then listen deeply:

- "Tell me what happened."
- "How is [the issue] affecting your work, your sleep, your ability to think?"

- "How is your heart?"
- "What emotions are washing over you?"
- "What are you achingly missing already?"
- What fond memories are at the forefront of your mind?"

You will likely get tears with the answer. That's OK. You've been courageous, have tenderly touched her heart and given the gift of your presence. You have loved her as Christ would.

What Do I Do About the Tears?

One of our greatest fears in providing authentic empathy is that the person we are with will start to cry. We do not want to make someone cry; it seems cruel or rude. **Please hear this alternative perspective**: these kinds of tears mean you have touched the person's heart. You have created a sacred place where *they are safe to cry*. That's a good thing! Stay in the moment. Do not fill it with words, just hold that space and let them cry. Just like my IHOP angel did. Sitting with someone who needs a good cry to express all of his or her pent-up emotions is *doing what love requires*. While it might make you (very) uncomfortable, it is a priceless gift. Let them see the compassion in your body language as you sit with hyper attention on them. It will be received with all the love intended.

We Are All Walking Wounded

My counselor son, Evan, tells me we form our perspective on life very early. "We all have scratches on our 'lens' through which we see the world. 'Scratches' come from the wounds in our life. They give us a distorted view of reality. Most of us have experienced a wound by the time we are three years old." Sobering.

What is a "wound"? It is anything that causes us to re-examine and redefine how we perceive ourselves, others, and God, and to see ourselves and others differently than God designed. Wounds warp our view of the world. They change the data we select to focus on, and the meaning we add to others' actions and words. It can be as small as harsh words from a person of influence to years-long physical, verbal, or emotional abuse.

For example, when children hear their parents are divorcing, they make up a story, run up their Ladder of Inference, and come to various conclusions about:

- **Themselves**: *It's my fault. I am not lovable. I'm not worthy of my father's/mother's devotion.*
- **Others**: *People can't be trusted. Love is never forever. To love is to get hurt.*
- **God**: *God's not real. He's not able to protect me. God abandons me when I need him the most.*[xxix]

Usually, we aren't conscious of taking on these false beliefs, but as we do, we interact with the world as if these lies are Truth. If I relate to those around me as if I am not worthy, not enough, alone, I will likely use dysfunctional behaviors to survive that truth. I might push people away when they get close, wanting to abandon them before they abandon me. I might become a perfectionist and think that if I make no mistakes, people won't discard me. I might cover up the pain associated with these beliefs by addictions to alcohol, drugs, or sex. There are excellent books on this topic, recommended at the end of this chapter, so I will not belabor it here. My point is **we are all the walking wounded to some extent**. We all carry false beliefs. We all exhibit dysfunctional behaviors—from people-pleasing to destructive addictions.[xxx]

Our adopted grandson, Judah, showed us just how early this can occur. Judah was late in talking. We all thought this was pretty normal since he had been exposed only to the Chinese Mandarin language his first 23 months of life. But his intuitive, brave dad had been pondering it and *asked.* Three months after his third birthday, Evan reflected to Judah, "You don't talk very much."

Judah nodded. "Why is that?" Evan wondered aloud. Judah answered immediately and surely, "Because of the *bad man.*" Now Evan, as a protective father, was all ears and wondered who he would have to hurt. "What bad man?" "The bad *doctor,*" Judah answered emphatically. "The bad doctor?" Evan encouraged. "Yes. He put me in the no-want-me box."

Evan was stunned. Judah had been left outside of a hospital, in a box, at ***three days old.*** Evan and Kim had never shared that with him. Had Judah heard stories about it at the orphanage? Could he have comprehended those stories as a child under 2? It seemed unlikely that the orphanage staff would use that terminology.

What false beliefs might Judah have embraced in his young mind? We can only guess. *I'm not wanted. I will be given away if I'm not good enough. Parents don't love their children. I can be abandoned at any moment. Doctors are not trustworthy. I am alone in the world and God can't protect me.*

Could a 3-day-old infant *sense* his unwanted-ness? What an astonishing phrase, "the no-want-me box". It brought tears to Evan's eyes. Judah, at three, was conscious of and able to articulate his wounded-ness.

Evan looked Judah straight in his eyes and promised, "Judah, Mommy and I will never put you in the no-want-me box." Evan told me he could see a weight lift from his son's small shoulders. A smile lit up Judah's sweet face as he threw his arms around Evan's neck and laughed with joy.

We are very grateful that Judah could tell us why he was withholding words and receive the Truth from his father—he need never fear abandonment. He now had new beliefs from which to interact in the world: *I am loved. I am cherished. I am safe. God saved me.*

> *He* [God] *heals the brokenhearted and binds up their wounds [healing their pain and Comforting them in their sorrow].* (Psalms 147:3 AMP)

Seeing Through God's Eye

What do wounds have to do with empathy? Just as we can make the choice to see another person's perspective, we can also choose to understand his or her struggle and to remember that we are all wounded people in need of love and grace. We can choose to **see each other through God's eyes**, see the brokenness in each other and therefore have empathy when others mess up or disappoint us. Loving one another requires us to provide the same bucket of grace to others, as we do for ourselves. These verses comfort and encourage me:

> *He* [God] *comes alongside us when we go through hard times, and before you know it, he brings us alongside someone else who is going through hard times so that we can be there for that person just as God was there for us.* (2 Corinthians 1:3-4 MSG)

> *Do not fear your weakness, for it is the stage on which My Power and My Glory performs most brilliantly.* Sarah Young, *Dear Jesus*, p. 18 based on 2 Corinthians 12:9

"I'm fine."

I adore Matthew West's song, *Truth Be Told.* Part of the refrain is:

I say, "I'm fine, yeah, I'm fine, oh, I'm fine, hey, I'm fine."
But I'm not, I'm broken

When someone tells me they're "fine," I believe it often means they're *not* fine. As in "My father died a month ago, we had to put our 13-year-old dog down last week, and our son just flunked out of college. But I'm fine." That's my signal to go into full-on empathy mode!

Perfect Empathy

In his beautiful book, *Imagine Heaven*, John Burke[xxxi] describes heaven as witnessed by people from all over the world and from all walks of life who have had near-death experiences. The communication method that these witnesses reported experiencing in heaven was "speaking" to others through telepathy. And as these folks were "listening", they "heard" as well, all the person's life experiences that formed their perspectives—quality empathy in every conversation. I can't wait!

Self-reflection

1. Which of the four empathetic practices do you want to enhance?
    - Take on his perspective
    - Stay out of judgment
    - Recognize his emotions
    - Acknowledge that you see those emotions (communicate)
2. What wounds are in your story? What false beliefs did you adopt as a result? What is the Truth?

3. How have wounds affected people in your family or friend circle? How does this (social) awareness change how you will view them?

Exercise

We all desire to be known and loved. If you truly want to know someone else's perspective, and see the world through his/her lens, ask one of these questions and then sit back and use hyper-focused listening. Be ready to share your own answer with appropriate vulnerability. Enjoy the deep connection!

- What is one of your significant life events?

- What are three events in your life that shaped who you are?
- Tell me your story.

Additional Reading

- *Draw Close to the Fire: Finding God in the Darkness*, Terry Wardle, Ph.D., 2004, Leafwood Publishing
- *It's OK That You're Not OK: Meeting Grief and Loss in a Culture That Doesn't Understand,* Megan Devine, 2017, Sounds True
- *Wounded: How to Find Wholeness and Inner Healing in Christ*, Terry Wardle, Ph.D., 2005, Leafwood Publishing

CHAPTER ELEVEN

LET PEACE BEGIN WITH ME

I have told you these things, so that in me you may have peace. In this world **you will have trouble.** *But take heart! I have overcome the world.* (John 16:33 NIV)

Alan Ahlgrim, pastor of Rocky Mountain Christian Church in Niwot, Colorado, surprised me one Sunday morning when he said, "Life is one conflict after another. If you are good at conflict, you are good at life."

My dictionary app defines conflict as "coming into collision or disagreement; being contradictory, at variance or in opposition; clash." Conflict is *any* perceived difference in opinion or course of action between two or more people. It covers an enormous range—everything from my husband and me not being able to agree on a fast-food restaurant—to the centuries' long fiery "disagreements" between Sunni and Shiite Muslims.

When you understand the breadth of what the word "conflict" encompasses, you see why life might look like one conflict after another. We live through days that are chock full of disagreements and differences of opinion, clashing values and contradictory viewpoints. Many conflicts seem small and are rather insignificant, like a minor bump in the road, while others absolutely rock our world. Suddenly, Pastor Alan's point resonated as truth. Life really is full of conflict—or trouble—as Jesus plainly stated in the verse above. And when we are in the midst of it, we may experience a love deficit! We need guidance in how to step into those challenging conversations with *compassion, kindness, humility, gentleness and patience. Bear*[ing] *with each other and forgiv*[ing] *one another.* (Colossians 3:10 NIV)

Pastor Alan pressed on. "Conflict is the price you pay for a *deeper relationship*." That was a new concept for me! I had thought that conflict pulled people apart, not drew them closer together.

To Avoid or Not to Avoid… That is the Question

Does conflict improve or hurt relationships? Are we stronger, better people and friends when we lean into it, or are we better off when we avoid it? Consider the following scenarios:

You have a co-worker who, at a meeting with your boss, shot down your brilliant proposal. Or you have a friend who offended you with her belittling comments about your faith. In either case, you were wounded, offended, and/or angry with that person. Well, let's face it—you were just plain mad. So now what?

Option One—Choose to avoid the conflict

Often our first reaction is to avoid the person. You're angry and hurt. Maybe it would be better to just give the offender a wide berth. It would be difficult to be civil at this point. Maybe you will approach him in a couple of days.

A day or two goes by. You think about confronting him, but that makes your blood boil, or has your stomach in somersaults. *It's probably pointless*, you justify. So, you avoid him some more. When you want to have someone join you for lunch, *his name* is last on your list.

More time goes by. Talking to him *now*, after all this time, would come across as petty and awkward. When forced to interact next, you choose to just pretend nothing happened. But in the meantime, what has happened to your relationship with that person? Has it grown deeper and closer?

Do you see how *avoiding* conflict has broken the relationship?

Option Two—Choose to step into the conflict

Consider the above scenarios again:

Your short-sighted coworker or your unkind friend offended you. However, instead of giving in to your first gut-level reaction, you choose to pause, check with the Holy Spirit, and then decide to approach the conflict. You make the choice to address the issue, courageously step into a hard conversation, and commit to work the conflict through to resolution. Now what has happened to your relationship? Is it still broken, or has it perhaps grown deeper and possibly even closer?

Do you see how leaning into conflict has the potential to improve and deepen your relationships?

Ponder the relationship you have with your spouse,

child or best friend. What conflicts have you had with them? While you may have initially avoided a hard conversation, I am guessing you eventually addressed it. And that's healthy! Over these 44 years of marriage my husband and I have had our share of conflict, but when we work through the hard conversations together we become closer and our relationship stronger. Our conflicts, while uncomfortable and unpleasant, have been crucial lessons in learning how to live at peace with each other.

If life is one conflict after another, and if knowing how to resolve conflict is necessary for peaceful, deep relationships, then we need to know what love requires in resolving conflict.

Jesus and Conflict

Lasting relationships require that you courageously choose to step into healthy conflict. Read that sentence again slowly and let that fact sink into your thoughts.

How do I know this is true? Well, the foremost reason is that Jesus said so.

> *If your fellow believer sins against you, you must go to that one privately and attempt to resolve the matter. If he responds, your*

> *relationship is restored. But if his heart is closed to you, then go to him again, taking one or two others with you.* (Matthew 18:15-17 TPT)

Jesus is clear in his directive. We are to "go"—we are to step into the discussion. The Apostle Paul concurs and provides more details.

> *Let your* **gentleness** *be evident to all.* [Even to those with whom you are in conflict] *The Lord is near. Do not be anxious about anything,* **but in every situation** [especially those pesky conflicts]***, by prayer and petition, with thanksgiving,*** *present your requests to God. And* **the peace of God,** *which transcends all understanding,* **will guard your hearts and your minds** *in Christ Jesus.* (Philippians 4:5-7 NIV, paraphrasing and emphasis mine)

Healthy conflict is really just learning how to disagree with others with an over-arching attitude of love. It requires gentleness and prayer and is part of the process God uses to mature and grow us as his sons and daughters.

> [God] gave us *teachers to equip his people for works of service, so that the body of Christ may be built up until we all reach unity in the faith and in the knowledge of the Son of God*

> *and become mature, attaining to the whole measure of the fullness of Christ. Then we will no longer be infants… Instead,* ***speaking the truth in love, we will grow to become in every respect the mature body*** *of him who is the head, that is, Christ.* (Ephesians 4:11-15 NIV emphasis mine)

Healthy conflict requires us to speak the truth—our perspective—in love instead of pretending there is no conflict.

What Does Healthy Conflict Sound Like?

The easiest way to have a hard conversation with *compassion, kindness, humility, gentleness, patience, and bearing with each other* is to **share *your* perspective in a way that shows your openness to hearing the *other* person's perspective**. We need all four aspects of Emotional Intelligence in order to do this well.

1. Self-Awareness
2. Social Awareness
3. Self-Expression
4. Relationship Management

Step One—Self-Awareness

The first step in healthy conflict is preparation; quiet, reflective time with the Holy Spirit is essential to gain clarity about what is at the heart of the issue for you. You do not have to ask yourself these questions in this order, but ask all of them and then listen for the Spirit's insights. Start with the category that's at the top of your mind. It always helps me to write my answers out.

1. **Values**–Which of your core values is dishonored or trampled?

2. **Emotions**–What emotions are swirling in you as you think about the situation?

3. **Data or Facts**–What did the person specifically *say or do* that triggered your emotions? If your answer begins with "I think" it's likely an assumption and not a fact.

4. **Thoughts and Assumptions**–When you heard what they said, or saw what they did, what did you think? What "story" did you make up in your head—what meaning did you add? What assumptions did you make?

5. **Physiology**–What went on in your body during the encounter? Was your jaw clenched? Were your shoulders tense? Could you sense your blood pressure rising?

6. **What do you desire or need from this conversation?** What would solve this conflict for you? What's an immediate next step, request, or suggestion you can make to move beyond the conflict?

Remember my co-worker, Jack, who triggered a values' meltdown in me at the beginning of the chapter on Values? My husband walked me through the questions above to help me understand what was happening in me. I knew I was furious with Jack, but I honestly didn't know why. My light-bulb moment was when Dave asked about what data I had, "What did Jack say?" Bingo! When Jack stated, ***"If*** you get that assignment done on time, we're going to knock the socks off the client," I ***perceived*** he was challenging my core value of Personal Responsibility. It was so freeing—such wonderful clarity—to recognize why I had such potent emotions. It was not a ***fact*** that he questioned my willingness to honor a deadline. I had added my meaning to his words, and had made up a story in my head, based on my core values.

Step Two—Social Awareness

Next, you want to walk through the six questions above a second time, and answer them how you think the *other* person would answer them. You are choosing empathy—to see the situation through the other person's eyes. You won't know all the answers and they're just best guesses, but you will be surprised how much it will help as you attempt to understand the person's perspective—and it just might lower your emotional response.

In my situation with Jack, as I reviewed the interaction through a social-awareness lens, I realized he probably wouldn't even remember saying that sentence. It wasn't one of the data points he would have selected in the conversation. He said it without malicious intent, just the way he'd expect me to say it to him since our team often had to motivate him to meet a deadline. His emotions when he hung up with me were likely delighted and pleased that we had connected. He would have had a very different perspective than mine.

So, after walking through Steps One and Two around the interaction with Jack, I realized there was no conflict.

Innocent words triggered me. Our relationship was in good shape, and I would greet him with a sincere hug next time I saw him. I had no thought or motive to avoid him; therefore, I had no need for a follow-up conversation with him.

Step Three—Self-Expression

> *Stop imitating the ideals and opinions of the culture around you, but be inwardly transformed by the Holy Spirit through a total reformation of how you think. This will empower you to discern God's will as you live a beautiful life, satisfying and perfect in his eyes.* (Romans 12:2 TPT)

Now that you have transformed your mind with the help of the Holy Spirit and have renewed clarity about your view and the other person's view, the next step is to communicate those perceptions with the other person. I call it stepping into healthy conflict. It takes prayer and courage, and it sounds something like this.

"Hey Kendall, yesterday when you said [exact phrase/data] in the meeting and I saw you roll your eyes [data], I thought you may have meant [thoughts and assumptions]. I have to confess, that made me [emotion words] especially since [core value] is so important to me. Would you be ok with [suggested improvement] next time?"

Back to the situation with Jack. If I believed he truly thought I wouldn't meet my obligation and that he didn't trust me, I would have stepped into a healthy conflict discussion. Here is what a conversation with Jack might have sounded like if it had been needed.

"Jack, I wanted to revisit our conversation from yesterday. When you said we would knock the socks off our client if I made the deadline, I made up in my head that you didn't trust that I would meet the deadline. How do you remember it?" I share my insights from my enhanced self-awareness (Step One) and then ask for his perspective (Step Two).

In these examples, I've stated how I saw the incident from *my perspective.* I've shown self-control and have called no one names or impugned their character. I've simply shared how the situation ***affected me***. I haven't implied that my assumptions were facts, I have calmly checked them out.

Step Four—Relationship Management

The last step to engage in conflict grounded in love is to ask for *the other person's perspective* and then use hyper-focused listening. "How did you see it? What am I missing?" You acknowledge that you know there *is* another perspective, that you respect her view of the situation and you are open to hearing it. She will probably provide more data, thoughts and values that you hadn't considered. You are humbly enrolling her in the solution. This is pure collaboration. Your stated intent is for a win-win outcome rather than having a winner (you) and a loser (her).

In a recent sermon, Jonathan Wiggins, pastor of Rez Church in Loveland, Colorado, shared that, "**Conflict is useful if your intent is to learn**." That is exactly what this approach fosters—learning about how each person sees the situation. The more complex the disagreement, the more you will want to dig into the other person's perspective—seek to understand it and learn with them how to move toward resolution.

Use the questions in Step One, above, and ask "What else?" after each initial response to be sure you unearth their full viewpoint.

- "What values were in play for you during the situation?" "What others?"
- "What emotions did you experience?" "What others?"

- "What thoughts ran through your mind?" "What else?"
- "What do you need?" "What else?"

The Results

Sometimes, your gentle explanation of your personal viewpoint in Step Three is a light-bulb moment for the other person and he'll say, "Oh, my goodness! That certainly wasn't my intent. I'm so sorry."

Other times, once you hear the other person's point of view (Step Four), it will surprise you how differently he saw it. He focused on completely different data, made different assumptions, or wanted to honor one of his own values. You may still disagree, but you will understand exactly how he came to a different opinion/conclusion when you hear it through his lens. You will have compassion and kindness toward him, even though you see it differently. That's a good time to find common ground and ask, "What do we agree on?"

Tips for Successful Conflict

- Stay attuned to the Holy Spirit

- Begin with the end goal in mind. How do you want the person to feel at the conclusion of your conversation? Let that goal guide your word choice and tone of voice.

- Keep it short and direct as opposed to long and subtle. It may seem "kinder" to do the latter, but the other person could easily miss your point and may innocently repeat her behavior since she didn't really comprehend your indirect, overly veiled message.

- Identify what you agree on, especially with a complex list of data and/or deep emotions.

The Steps in Action

I recall a recent situation that had me stoked and ready for a conflict with my husband. We were on vacation with another couple, and David said something to the husband that I thought was completely inappropriate and offensive. I stood there speechless, stunned and furious—and David could see it. I didn't notice a vehement reaction on the face of our friend, but out of sheer embarrassment, to distance myself from Dave's words, and without a pause to listen to the Holy Spirit, I murmured something under my breath to our friend. David caught it and looked equally mad at me.

Now, mind you, one reason I married David was because he is a true gentleman, so I was even more appalled. I had such a strong emotional reaction that I *knew* I needed to do a bit of soul searching before I spoke to him. When I was calmer, I walked through the six questions (page 190) to enhance my self-awareness (Step One). As I wrote out what had happened inside of me during the incident, I was *convinced* that I had a solid case to be justifiably upset.

I honestly tried to consider Dave's viewpoint (Step Two), but for the life of me, I couldn't imagine what he had been thinking and feeling. I was struggling with empathy.

Two days later, when we were both more composed, I shared my *perspective* with him (Step Three). My description included the sentence that had triggered me, the values that I felt were disrespected, and my emotions and thoughts. Then I did a mic-drop in my head, feeling a bit self-righteous. I knew I needed to listen to his perspective (Step Four), but I have to admit, I thought nothing else needed to be said. Just being honest!

As I stood there still a bit smug, David **added data** I hadn't previously known about something that had occurred between this friend and him in the past. It *totally* *changed* what I thought I had witnessed. I suddenly understood his motive and his words (which I noticed, as I reviewed the scene in my mind again, hadn't been spoken in anger). I now saw the interaction in a whole different light. The conflict between David and I, that I thought would be intense, was over almost as soon as it began. It was truly that simple. When I understood the interaction from his perspective it wiped away the story I had told myself in my head.

> Resolving conflict is rarely about who is right. It is about acknowledgement and appreciation of differences. adapted from *The Magic of Conflict*

The Apostle Paul and Jesus' brother, James, describe the attitude we should seek in every healthy conflict conversation.

> *Do nothing out of selfish ambition or vain conceit. Rather, in humility value others* [and their perspectives] *above yourselves, not looking to your own interests but each of you to the interests of the others.* (Philippians 2:3-4 NIV, bracketed note mine) *Real wisdom, God's wisdom, begins with a holy life and is characterized by getting along with others. It* [a holy life] *is gentle and reasonable, overflowing with mercy and blessings, not hot one day and cold the next,*

> *not two-faced. You can develop a healthy, robust community that lives right with God and enjoy its results only if you* ***do the hard work of getting along with each other, treating each other with dignity and honor.*** (James 3:17-18 MSG)

Timing is Everything

> *Go ahead and be angry. You do well to be angry—but don't use your anger as fuel for revenge. And don't stay angry. Don't go to bed angry. Don't give the Devil that kind of foothold in your life.* (Eph 4:26-27 MSG)

When I am out of synch with someone I do not sleep well, so I prefer to wrestle a conflict to the ground before the sun goes down—and be obedient to the Word. But in my hurry, I have rushed tough conversations before cooling down and processing my thoughts and emotions. That doesn't end well. Conversely, my husband wants time to process, even if that means waiting a day or two before resolving a conflict. We've had conflict about when to have conflict!

In the verse above, Paul implores us to not *stay angry*. Rather, to address the conflict as soon as possible; Our lives are best—more abundant—when we are at peace with everyone. Stepping into healthy conflict, as soon as we have calmed down and conducted a self-assessment, will give us that peace. And my trust in people goes up when *they* have the courage to tell me when there is an obstacle between us. Coming to me within 24 hours lets me know they are committed to identifying and resolving the barrier in order to restore the equilibrium with our connection.

If we stew too long on the offense, *the Devil gets a foothold* that he eagerly turns into *fuel for revenge*, unforgiveness or a broken relationship. You now have the tools you need to prepare for a conflict conversation within a day's time. Put on your Respond-ability cape and go for it!

A Core Values Conflict

When your perspective is based on a core value, you will likely find yourself in a conflict mode called competing. It's a win-lose approach. Paul has an admonition:

> *But avoid foolish controversies and genealogies and arguments and quarrels about the law, because these are unprofitable and useless.* ***Warn a divisive person once, and then warn them a second time.*** *After that, have nothing to do with them. You may be sure that such people are warped and sinful; they are self-condemned.* (Titus 3:9-11 NIV)

I envision Paul's advice here is about a core values' conflict.

There are plenty of clashes around core values in our culture today. An example would be discussing my passionate pro-life stand with my equally passionate abortion-rights' activist friend. We are miles apart in our thinking and values. I want to understand how she came to her opinion, and I want her to feel respected. But it's unlikely that I will change her mind or that she can change mine since we are discussing those things that are at our core. We have opposing positions of the heart. It's "unprofitable and useless." So, we avoid that topic and focus on what we agree on.

When a person's stance is opposite the Word of God, which is absolute Truth, it's a heart issue for the Holy Spirit to address, not a dispute on which you can collaborate. Present your perspective with kindness and respect, listen to the other person's perspective and then leave amicably with a prayer on your lips, releasing the "conflict" to God.

If you find yourself returning to the same conflict with the same person, examine the values that are in play and how important it is to agree or not. If your positions or values are at opposite ends, but you really want to preserve the relationship, then it will be wise to focus your conversations on areas in which you agree. On the other hand, if you are an accountant who values honesty and integrity, and you continue to find yourself in weekly disputes with your boss who wants you to cook the books, this is probably a time to seek another job rather than step into conflict over and over.

Collaboration

The most effective mode of communication to resolve a conflict is collaboration. Together you pool your different views of the situation, add each other's data to the interpretation of events, separate fact from assumptions, analyze the values involved and name the emotions at play. This is one of our choices for love that does takes an investment in time. It is always worth it. It will deepen your relationships and grow God-honoring fruit: *compassion, kindness, humility, gentleness and patience*. You will be obedient to your Lord *serving others, humbly, with love*.

Self-reflection

1. What practice could you adopt to improve your conflict conversations?

2. Ask the Holy Spirit with whom you may be in a values clash. What are your next steps?

3. Read Ephesians 4. How do Paul's words inform the way you want to step into conflict?

Exercises

1. Use Step One—Self-awareness to gain clarity on what happened between you and a person you are avoiding. Craft words to share with him/her. How would that conversation positively change the relationship?

2. Next time your negative emotions rise, pause, listen to the Holy Spirit, and apply the Four Steps.

Additional Reading

- *The Anatomy of Peace: Resolving the Heart of Conflict,* The Arbinger Institute. 2008, Arbinger Properties, Inc.

- *Crucial Conversations: Tools for Talking When the Stakes are High*, Kerry Patterson and Joseph Grenny, Ron McMillan and Al Switzler. 2011, McGraw-Hill Education; 2nd edition

CHAPTER TWELVE

SPEAK THE TRUTH IN LOVE

Do you ever wish you could tell someone exactly what you are thinking?

- Terell would be so much more effective if he wasn't so negative.
- My spouse shoots down my ideas leaving me so devalued.
- Doesn't Dara see all the eyes roll when she is monopolizing the conversation?

We all have suggestions for the people in our lives, but we often keep them to ourselves. Frankly, it's appropriate and socially healthy not to say *everything* that pops into our heads. But many times, speaking this kind of truth in love is exactly what love requires. It gets back to the question: *to avoid or not to avoid.* If I avoid speaking about the issues in the bullets above, I may distance myself from those people or even come to resent them—damaging the relationship rather than building it up.

Providing Feedback

Giving unsolicited feedback—speaking the truth in love—can appear like conflict, whether you are providing it or receiving it. But just as conflict is the price you pay for deeper relationships, feedback is the price you pay for more *trusting* relationships.

I was in a beautiful hotel ballroom for the opening cocktail event of a year-long leadership training program. It was my first introduction to the participants—each selected for their high potential as future leaders in their organization. As they wandered in, I was struck by how much pressure they were under. It's always challenging to walk into a roomful of strangers by yourself, overly conscious of the first impression you want to make. I greeted each one with a welcoming handshake and noted their names. As Xavier was asking me questions about the program, I suddenly realized I had a choice to make. Do I provide this person *I just met* with unsolicited feedback or not? I knew what love required. I leaned in and whispered in his ear, "Your zipper is down."

Xavier still tells that story with a hearty laugh eight years later! I had earned his trust. As embarrassing as it was for both of us, I did him a service by preventing repeated embarrassment throughout the evening. Imagine if he had excused himself to the restroom an hour later and realized that NO ONE had had the courtesy to tell him. His trust in his new cohort would be gone.

Having the courage to tell a person about something that is tripping him up, or an unintended impact he is having, is *serving him, humbly, with* love and you can do it with *compassion and kindness.*

How do you provide feedback so people receive it well? Kim Scott, in her excellent book, *Radical Candor*[xxxii], has a simple formula. She says to provide it with directness and caring. Don't beat around the bush, get right to the point, and let your words and tone of voice communicate that your intent is to serve—not to humiliate or demean. The person should hear that you want to bring out the best in her and for her.

I use these three steps. You will hear some of the same principles we learned about in the last chapter.

1. Succinctly and specifically describe what you heard or saw. Just the facts. Your feedback will

also be better received if you provide it sooner rather than later.

2. Explain the impact on you—express your thoughts, emotions or values. The incident must be something that you witnessed personally. Starting with, "Alex told me you did so-and-so," is not effective.

3. Make a suggestion for improvement or solicit the other person's ideas for a change.

Let's use the situations listed at the opening of this chapter as examples.

The negative co-worker

Me: Terell, yesterday when we were talking about the changes to the budget process you said, "There is no way they'll ever work." When I heard that, it made me think you didn't have hope or trust in our budget department. I could hear your concerns better if you would share specific areas that you think need more attention. What do you think?

OR

Me: Terell, yesterday when we were talking about the

changes to the budget process you said, "There is no way they'll ever work." Did you notice a few people in the room roll their eyes?

Terell: No.

Me: I did and it made me concerned about what assumptions folks might have made. I want you to be perceived as the problem-solver you are. What if you shared your specific concerns or alternative solutions when you are feeling negative about a proposal?

I am being very direct, specific and concise, and I am hoping that Terell hears in my choice of words and tone of voice that I care about him being respected, heard and valued.

The spouse who shoots down ideas

Me: Honey, as we were talking about the design of the new barn before lunch, you interrupted me when I was explaining the type of windows I wanted. Then you changed the subject to the color of the roof. It felt like you didn't value my opinion. When would you be ready to hear my ideas?

OR

Me: Honey, as we were talking about the design of the new barn before lunch, you interrupted me when I was explaining the type of windows I wanted. Then you changed the subject to the color of the roof. How best can I get my thoughts into the process?

The friend who monopolizes the conversation

Me: Dara, last Wednesday when we all went out to lunch at P.F. Chang's you shared about your trip to Mexico for about 20 minutes. Then when Sloan and Jen talked about their upcoming trips, you interrupted them and shared more about your trip to Mexico. Did you notice that?

Dara: I guess I didn't.

Me: I know you get really excited to share your stories when you are with us. I wanted to mention it because I was sorry that I didn't get to hear much from Jen and Sloan. How do you think we can balance the conversation better next time?

OR

Me: Dara, last Wednesday when we all went out to lunch at P.F. Chang's you shared about your trip to Mexico for about 20 minutes. Then when Sloan and Jen talked about their upcoming trips, you interrupted them and shared more about your trip to Mexico. Did you notice that?

Dara: I remembered that I had forgotten to mention a few things, and I needed to get them out before I forgot.

Me: I've been there! I wanted to mention it because I saw Sloan's and Jen's facial expressions. They seemed hurt and I know you wouldn't want to have that impact on them. I wonder if at our next lunch you might let them share their updates first.

Do you hear the directness and the caring? As with our conflict discussions, you do not want to be vague in order to protect the person's feelings—that's not the "caring" I am talking about. You might end up being so vague that Dara doesn't get the message and then she loses the opportunity to change her behavior.

The goal is for the feedback to be useful—clear enough that the person can choose a specific behavior to change for the good. It wouldn't be very useful to Terell, my husband, or Dara for me to say that they were rude, disrespectful or annoying. 1) Those are judgmental words and can close their ears to your message, and 2) it doesn't help them understand how to solve the problem or what you'd like to see as the solution.

Specific Feedback to Someone You Hardly Know

Some of us find it uncomfortable to give feedback to the people we know. We are afraid it will damage the relationship. Others think it's more uncomfortable to provide feedback to someone we hardly know or to someone who doesn't work directly for us. Let me share Greg's story.

At another mixer for a different leadership program, I watched a tall man walk up and join a small group's conversation. After he spoke for a few minutes, I noticed members of the group begin to slip away. The man, Greg, soon found himself alone so he sought another small group, only to have the same thing happen. This was repeated a third time.

The next day, Greg showed up for his scheduled one-on-one review with me of his 360° Assessment which was an evaluation of his work performance and presence by those above him in his organization, his peers, the people who worked for him and his customers. Greg named several take-aways from the feedback, and identified a few items he intended to work on, but he never mentioned that the word "arrogant" appeared multiple times in the open notes section.

I asked the Holy Spirit for wisdom and courage, and dove in. "Greg, what do you think about the word 'arrogant' to describe you?" Without missing a beat, he explained matter-of-factly, "I've heard that for years! I'm the best [his profession] in the world."

Greg had added his meaning to the word, "arrogant" and thought people called him that because of his world-renowned expertise. "Can you be the best in the world and be humble?" I asked. He paused, deep in thought, and finally said, "I guess I don't know what they mean by 'arrogant'". So, I told him what I had observed the night before. I gave him concise, specific, direct information in a tone of voice that communicated that I was on his side.

"Greg, you are quite tall, and when you speak with people, you stand very close to them. This means they have to look straight up at you and you are looking down your nose at them. You also have a way of chucking your chin [I demonstrated]. As I was observing you last night, I didn't hear you ask about the others; instead, you spent your time doing all the talking." Greg was fascinated. No one had ever explained to him the actual behaviors that others might perceive as "arrogant." He found that hearing the truth in love was so helpful, he wanted me to be his personal coach and give him *more* useful feedback!

I have a wonderful example of *receiving* feedback from a stranger who loved me enough to tell me the truth during a business trip to Philadelphia. My Uber pulled up in front of a beautiful, historic hotel. A uniformed doorman who looked like a palace guard in London, opened the door and greeted me with a gigantic smile.

The next morning, showered, and in one of my favorite suits, I confidently strode through the lobby on my walk to the client's training facility. The same "palace guard" with the sweeping red overcoat was holding the door open. I passed through and flashed him a smile of appreciation, along with a cheery "Good morning!" Before I knew what was happening, he had my upper arm in his grasp and pulled me close to whisper in my ear, "You have lipstick on your teeth." Surprised and grateful, I responded with the joy of the Lord, "Thank you! You're the best!" *That's a man I can trust.*

People are hungry for the truth when we share it with a sincere desire to help them be their best.

Receiving Feedback

What if you are the feedback receiver? Feedback, even when it's delivered very well, can hurt. When receiving it a person can be gracious or resistant, grateful or offended—and they can choose to change or not. Our role as the feedback provider is to give the person the truth to help them be more effective or appreciated. Ideally, they will receive it that way—as new information (data) that they use or not.

What did Greg do with his additional information? He received it well. He spent the entire year working on his presence. At the conclusion of the program, the class voted him best member of the cohort. He chose the path of receiving feedback graciously and changed. He is a role model for me!

When you are on the receiving end of feedback, there's one simple response that love requires, "Thank you." Even though it hurts and even though you may not agree with the person's perspective, you are thanking him for having the courage to come to you directly with information that may serve you. You certainly can say, "Let me think about that. Can I call you if I have some questions?" Then, in concert with the Holy Spirit, you decide what to do with the information provided.

Do not justify your behavior—as tempting as that is! You will make the person who had the courage to come to you less likely to approach you in the future. I *want* people to be comfortable approaching me with problems or concerns. I can't correct a poor impression unless I know about it! If I am tripping up or offending others, I want to know it and grow from it. I seek to be the feedback *receiver* who, through my relaxed body language, open tone of voice and Holy Spirit-inspired response, makes the giver of the feedback glad they came to me.

Early in my work with CI International, my boss, Jon, came to me with feedback that was hard to hear. "Elle, in our company meeting last week when you said, 'I don't read the profit-and-loss statements. They're just Greek to me,' you gave me the impression that you aren't bright enough to understand them, or you don't care about the company's financial position. I don't think that's true, and I want you to be accurately perceived as the smart woman I know you are. How could you better communicate what's behind your thinking?" Whew. That was truth that stung. I said, "Thank you. Let me think on that."

Embarrassed, but also grateful, I now had the chance to consider my words and change the impression my boss—and probably my peers—had about me. Jon was open and direct with me, and I clearly heard that he cared about my reputation in the company. That's SO much better than having my reputation sullied and not knowing it. Love does exist in the workplace!

> For the want of feedback, residue accumulated.
> Because residue built up, trust was lost. For the want of trust, working together became difficult.
> Because working together was difficult, decisions were avoided.
> For the want of making decisions, the business failed.
> And all for the want of feedback.
>
> *Thomas G. Crane*

What Never Works

The following practices will absolutely destroy healthy conflict and effective feedback—whether you are on the giving or receiving end. You may have grown up hearing or seeing these approaches used in your family or among friends, so now they may be what you do. Or perhaps you imagine that they more accurately convey your emotions. Sometimes, we might even assume we *must* use them in order to be true to who we are. But they are destructive—they damage relationships instead of deepening them. We need the Holy Spirit's help to overcome these caustic communication tendencies since none of them show *compassion, kindness, humility, gentleness* or *patience.*

1. **Destructive Words**

When we engage in using harsh, disparaging words, we are choosing to *act out* our emotions rather than the healthier practice of *naming* our emotions. In the heat of the moment, it might be tempting to use an expletive to express our anger or frustration, but that's not choosing love.

If this habit slips into your arguments, make a firm decision to eradicate it. Use Appendix B that lists our Feeling and Emotion Words to better understand what you are experiencing. This will enable you to communicate more calmly and clearly so that you can accurately convey your emotions without harsh or hurtful words.

2. **Name Calling**

Starting your conflict discussion with "You idiot!" "What a knuckle-headed thing to do!" or worse, will not motivate the other person to want to join a collaborative discussion toward an amicable solution. Remember, love requires us to be kind, not arrogant or rude.

3. Assigning Motive

When we ascribe or label the other person's perceived motive it destroys a loving attitude and conversation. "You're so irresponsible!" is not nearly as useful, compassionate or gentle as stating your non-judgmental, fact-based perspective: "When you showed up 30 minutes late for our lunch (fact) it made me think (thought) that I am not very important to you (value)."

4. Exaggerated Words

"You never," and "You always," are two phrases that reveal our biases, our reflexive loops, and are not truth. They may *feel* completely true but exaggerating an accusation will not open another person's ears to your point of view. They will write you off as irrational—someone with whom they certainly do not want to connect or collaborate.

5. Harsh Body Language and Tone of Voice

When you look scary and raise your voice, I am not inclined to want to change my behavior or step into healthy conflict with you! Part of taking time to cool off before engaging in the conversation is about garnering more self-control through the help of the Holy Spirit. Then you can authentically join the conversation—respond to the stimulus—with an open body posture and a calm, rational quality to your voice. And you will show love by "*valuing others above yourself.*"

When you catch yourself using any of these behaviors, take a deep breath, apologize, and let your listener know you need some time to cool your emotions and gain perspective about what is really going on. That's demonstrating self-control, the fruit of the Spirit.

> *Lay aside bitter words, temper tantrums, revenge, profanity, and insults. But instead be kind and affectionate toward one another.* (Ephesians 4:31 TPT)

Using a Third Party

One way some of us "avoid" conflict or feedback is to tell Henry about the problem we have with Cliff. The third person, Henry in this example, is used as a *substitute* for direct communication to Cliff, or as a conduit to Cliff. I don't have the courage to go directly to Cliff, so I am hoping Henry will. Unfortunately, this is an excellent way to sabotage a relationship—with both

Henry and Cliff. It's not doing what love requires. Henry now trusts you less (because you talk about people behind their backs), you haven't been humble and honest enough to go to Cliff directly, and you have denied Cliff the opportunity to share *his* perspective or to make it right.

If you need help or coaching in how to approach Cliff, an *appropriate* third party can be helpful. Choose a trustworthy, loving person who is skilled in conflict. I use my wise husband as the third party for this purpose. He can coach me through my self-awareness process, pray with me as I seek social awareness and empathy, and then challenge me with, "When will you have this conversation with Cliff?"

What If I Get It Wrong?

It's genuine emotional and spiritual maturity to accept that you will fail. Of course, you'll get conflict and feedback wrong—you're human! I regularly mess up challenging conversations. As someone who prefers thinking by speaking, I can suddenly notice that the wrong words have poured from my mouth! Did I say that out loud?

I recommend three things:

1. When responding to a difficult situation, exercise the muscle that closes your mouth long enough to check in with the Holy Spirit—that self-control pause.
2. In that pause, ask God how he wants you to respond. This is also a time where he may reveal areas in which you need to grow and mature.
3. Read the next chapter on forgiveness. We have a saying in our family, "It's not whether you mess up, it's how you correct it that counts." And a friend of mine says it this way, "If you make a mess, clean it up."

Self-reflection

1. What concept most resonated with you?

2. What practice in giving or receiving feedback will you add?

3. What communication habits or behaviors do you have that "never work"? Ask the Holy Spirit to work in your heart so that you can let go of those detrimental habits.

Exercise

What person has the Spirit laid on your heart who needs

to hear direct, caring truth from you. Pray for wisdom and courage and write out what you want to say using the three steps, above. Use a caring, open body language and a kind tone of voice to deliver the message.

Additional Reading

- *Radical Candor*, Kim Scott. 2019, St. Martin's Press

CHAPTER THIRTEEN

CHOOSE FORGIVENESS

Forgiveness is a necessary and natural next topic. Since I have stimulated thoughts about past wounds and current conflicts, the Spirit may have brought someone to your mind—someone you need to forgive or from whom you should ask forgiveness. Remember our family saying, "It's not whether you mess up, it's how you correct it that counts"? My husband and I wanted our children to learn that offenses and failures are inevitable in this life, *but then what?*

Forgiveness—seeking it, receiving it, and giving it—is the simple yet profound answer. Bestselling author of *Simple Reminders*, Bryant H. McGill[xxxiii] makes it clear. "There is no love without forgiveness, and there is no forgiveness without love."

Our Marching Orders

While choosing forgiveness can be very difficult, it is an act of love, and to be obedient servants of Christ, it's one we have to choose—often. Here's what Jesus said.

> *For if you forgive others their trespasses [their reckless and willful sins], your heavenly Father will also forgive you. But if you do not forgive others [nurturing your hurt and anger with the result that it interferes with your relationship with God], then your Father will not forgive your trespasses.* (Matthew 6:14-15 AMP)

His disciple, Peter, later asked for more clarification.

> *"Lord, how many times will my brother sin against me and I forgive him and let it go? Up to seven times?" Jesus answered him, "I say to you, not up to seven times, but 70 times seven."* (Matthew 18: 21 AMP)

Commenting on this verse, Dr. David Stoop, author of *Forgiving What You'll NEVER Forget,* magnifies this noting that, "One ancient manuscript added the words 'a day'."[xxxiv] That would mean **490 times per day** or over 178,850 times a year! It sounds like there is no limit to forgiving.

In his New Testament letters, the Apostle Paul reminds us:

> *Be kind and compassionate to one another, forgiving each other, just as in Christ God forgave you.* (Ephesians 4:32 NIV)

> *Bear with each other and forgive one another if any of you has a grievance against someone. Forgive as the Lord forgave you. And over all these virtues put on love, which binds them all together in perfect unity.* (Colossians 3:13-14 NIV)

When we mess up, we need to ask forgiveness; when others mess up, we must extend forgiveness to them. Why? Because that's how God has treated us. Yet granting forgiveness is one of the toughest things to do. Why is that?

Forgiveness Facts

In his highly readable and practical book, Dr. Stoop[xxxv] unpacks the truth about forgiving. I found myself much more open and prepared to forgive after absorbing his wisdom. Here are four truths that had the greatest impact on my attitude toward forgiveness.

1. **Forgiving is *not* forgetting.**[xxxvi] As humans, we can't possibly forget what happened. Whew! This

has been a roadblock to me. I thought I had not fully forgiven someone if I remembered what she did to me. We *can* forgive and we *will* remember. We are not capable of erasing memories. What I have noticed is that the memory of the event softens after I forgive.

2. **Forgiving is *not* excusing the offender's behavior.**[xxxvii] What makes forgiveness hard for me is that I think I have to respond with, "Yeah, it's fine," when I am thinking, *NO IT'S NOT!* The offender *will* be judged—just not by me. Forgiveness does not mean the offender is free of consequences. We just won't be the one doling out those consequences. That's up to earthly courts and our heavenly Father. The only consequence we have control over is reconciliation. See #4, below.

3. **Forgiving is between God and me.**[xxxviii] I do not have to go to an offender (who may actually be a danger to me) to tell him, "I forgive you." Forgiveness is first and foremost a conversation with God where I hand the burden of justice and punishment over to him. Rather than clench unforgiveness in my hand, I tell God that I trust him to deal with my perpetrator in a way only

God can—he knows the heart and motives of the person far better than I do and he has the power to make it right.

I've often bristled at people who say, "You need to let it go!" That felt to me like I was letting the offense drop into an empty well, never to be heard of again. Now I understand that it's not falling out of my hands, unaddressed. Instead, I **place it in God's hands**. And when I release it to God, I also let go of bitterness, anger and resentment. I am free.

4. **Forgiving is *not* reconciling.**[xxxix] Reconciling, according to the Oxford Dictionary, is "the restoring of friendly relations." That I can forgive but not restore "friendly relations" was a game-changer for me. I had thought that if I forgave someone, I was also saying they could stay in my life; that we would somehow magically return to a healthy relationship. There are many situations where it's **absolutely not healthy** to be in a relationship with your offender, so understanding that forgiveness and reconcil-iation are distinct is critical.

Forgiveness is something I can choose to do

regardless of what my offender does. It's a one-way transaction. But reconciliation is between two parties and both have to agree. I have to want to reconcile with you and you have to want to be reconciled with me. If one party doesn't choose to reconcile, there's no restoration of the relationship.

Bottom-line: I can forgive my wrongdoer by giving the responsibility for punishment to God. ***Then* I can choose** to restore the relationship or not.

The Pain is Real

Before I share a formula for your forgiveness conversation with God, I want to help you acknowledge and deal with the enormous hurdle of grief. Just as in the chapter on Authentic Empathy, in order to have authentic forgiveness you have to confront your emotions first, *then* the facts, *then* the solution.

You experienced a wound—an event or an interaction that caused emotional anguish—and possibly deep, long, painful suffering. God knows this and invites us to lament—to cry, weep, howl, wail, moan, and grieve. Forgiveness will be nearly impossible without addressing your emotional pain first.

Did you know that in the Book of Psalms, or songs, there are more Psalms of Lament than Psalms of Praise? This is because emotional pain is a common and weighty aspect of the human condition. A lamentation is an oral or written expression of sorrow, mourning, or regret. **We need to accurately and completely express our physical and emotional pain before we can sincerely move to forgiveness.** The lamentations in the Psalms follow a simple pattern that we can borrow:

1. **Beginning**: stepping into a conversation with God and a plea for his divine help.
2. **Complaint**: saying what you lost through the ordeal, what it cost you, and even your frustrations with God. Get it all out. This is often the longest section.
3. **Confidence**: acknowledge that God has heard your complaint and will respond accordingly.
4. **Praise God**: for his faithfulness to answer your pleas.

If you are dealing with an offense and its subsequent grief, you likely need to authentically lament before you can move on to forgiveness. There is an excellent exercise at the end of this chapter that will help you.

Forgiveness Conversation with God

Allow your lamentation to steep in your soul. Ask the Holy Spirit to help you let go of that longing to punish the offender. You do not want to rush only to have an insincere conversation with God. You may have to read through your lamentation many times, add to it, or read it to a trusted friend or pastor before you have adequately grieved.

You may never "feel" like forgiving. Researchers tell us that "feelings *follow* actions."[xl] When we take an action, like obediently *acting* lovingly toward others, eventually the *feeling* of love will follow. Similarly, when you take the *action* of expressing your grief to God, the feeling of freedom will follow, and you can authentically release your need to punish into God's almighty hands. You will be capable of experiencing sincere forgiveness and inner joy. You will experience freedom from the bitterness and anger that has been eating you up.

Here's a simple prayer to forgive others. Please elaborate to fit your prayer style:

1. "I forgive [name] who [the offensive action]"

2. "She/he caused me much pain and [list emotions]."

3. "I release to you any judgment and punishment I have been counting on for [name] in my heart."

4. "I submit [name] and my unforgiveness to you."

It might sound like this: "Father, I forgive Brent who sexually harassed me to the point of choosing to leave the job I loved. He embarrassed and belittled me. I was powerless, depressed, and angry. Lord, I release to you the punishment I have been wanting for Brent. I submit Brent and my unforgiveness before your throne."

It is as simple and profound as the prayer of reconciliation you prayed to invite Jesus into your life. Dr. Stoop concedes that withholding forgiveness "can never replace what has been destroyed."[xli] But the excess brain capacity you have been using to stockpile your anger, and the places in your body where you have been hoarding your bitterness are now replaced with God's peace and are available for loving others. *The peace of God, which transcends all understanding* (Philippians 4:7 NIV), will follow and you will be able to offer *compassion, kindness, humility, gentleness and patience* to those around you.

A Forgiveness Story

For ten years I had distanced myself from a Christian friend who had broken my trust. I worked hard to forgive her, but at the time, I didn't feel safe going to her and declaring, "I forgive you." I also mistakenly believed that reconciliation went hand-in-hand with true forgiveness. Wanting to protect myself, I wasn't ready to restore the relationship. The unforgiveness hung heavy on my heart. The years had lessened the weight slightly, but I still felt its presence.

One Sunday morning at a church neither of us had known the other was attending, God put her directly in my path. I was unnerved and anxious. She seemed to want to pick up right where we had left off—acting as if we were fully reconciled. I wasn't ready. My mind screamed, "Protect yourself!" I needed to determine whether she was the same person who had wounded me so deeply a decade earlier. So, I asked to meet her for coffee. I can still remember how fearful and anxious I was on the drive there. I prayed for courage and the right words the whole way.

After our initial hellos, I got right to the point. With a trembling voice I asked, "Do you remember what happened with [the situation]?" "I do," she replied, "that was horrible. Can you forgive me?" We embraced in tears as I said, "Yes." As we caught up over the next hour, I realized she wasn't the same person. The Holy Spirit had softened her heart and taken her on a valuable journey of self-reflection and growth. I was ready to go beyond forgiveness to reconciliation. For the past eight years, she's been one of my most loyal, kind, and generous friends, and I have happily worked to be the same friend for her. With God, all things are possible!

Asking Forgiveness from Others

I think we can do better than, "I'm sorry," when we have offended someone. A heartfelt, "I'm sorry," works fine when you spill the milk, bump into someone on the street or forget to stop at the store for groceries. But **when your offense results in emotional distress for another person** such as when you betray a confidence, act as a stumbling stone in someone's Christian walk, or cheat on your spouse, love requires something more than a simple "I'm sorry."

I think the following short formula combined with a conversation with the Holy Spirit will increase your ownership in the wrongdoing and will inspire gratitude in the recipient—if not immediate absolution.

1. "[Name of the person who you damaged], I [specifically what you did]"

2. "I believe you must have felt [name an emotion you likely caused]."

3. "I was wrong. Can you forgive me?" [Pause and allow the person time to receive your words and reflect.]

Here's how it might sound: "Erin, I betrayed your confidence and shared with Alexa our conversation about your marriage challenges. I imagine you are humiliated, crushed, and angry, and your trust in me was broken. I was terribly wrong to share that. Can you forgive me? (pause) Can I begin to earn back your trust?"

The first question is about forgiveness, the second is about reconciliation. I am conceding that Erin may forgive me, but at this point she may be very hesitant to reconcile.

Gulp! Does this take vulnerability, courage, and humility? Absolutely. It takes the power of the Holy Spirit to do it well. And while it comes with those costs, think of the impact. You have truly been obedient in *serving others humbly in love*. What is the impact on Erin? It supplies some of the restitution she may expect. You've owned your offense; acknowledged it for the depth of pain it caused and admitted that she may not want to continue a close friendship with you. You've made an admirable choice to humble yourself and do the hard work that love requires.

Rather than tossing a quick, "I'm sorry," over your shoulder, sincerely acknowledging the wrong you committed and asking for forgiveness demonstrates the love of Christ and *clothes [you] with compassion, kindness, humility, gentleness and patience.*

While the intent of this book is to give you tools to love other humans to a greater extent, I think using this formula in asking *God's* forgiveness is what he desires from us as well. Mercifully, he forgets.

> *For You, O Lord, are good, and ready to forgive [our sins, sending them away, completely letting them go forever and ever].* (Psalms 86:5 AMP)

Forgiving Yourself

Forgiving yourself may be the hardest form of forgiveness. I am not equipped to do service to this topic, but I mention it here because *carrying* this form of unforgiveness **diminishes your capacity to love others**. If you suspect that you have not forgiven yourself for an offense, even if you received forgiveness from the person you hurt, please consider speaking with a counselor and/or pastor. Carlos Whittaker, in his book *Enter Wild*,[xlii] shares his long journey toward forgiving himself, and Dr. Stoop's book also covers the topic well. Both are recommended at the end of this chapter.

Self-reflection

1. What has this chapter stirred up in you? Ask God what he wants your next step to be.

2. What makes forgiving those who have hurt you so hard?

3. With these truths revealed, who has the Holy Spirit laid on your heart to work toward forgiving? Will it be a conversation between you and God, or do you also want to reconcile with that person?

Exercises

1. Read how David poured out his grievances and emotions in Psalms 55, 56 and 70. I strongly recommend The Message version of the Bible for this exercise. Read these psalms aloud with your most dramatic voice (like when David was making his plea to God).

2. Write your expression of pain, a lamentation, addressing a situation God has laid on your heart. Use the template provided for us in the Psalms.

   Beginning: stepping into a conversation with God and a plea for divine assistance.

   Complaint: explaining what you lost through the ordeal, what it cost you, your frustrations with God. Get it all out. This should be the longest section.

   Confidence: acknowledge that God has heard the complaint and will respond accordingly.

   Praise God: for his faithfulness to answer your pleas.

Additional Reading

- *Enter Wild*, Carlos Whittaker 2020 Waterbrook/Random House
- *Forgiving What You'll Never Forget,* David Stoop, Ph.D. 2003, Revell Books

CHAPTER FOURTEEN

LOVE WHO?!

> *But I say to you who hear, love your enemies and do something wonderful for them in return for their hatred. When someone curses you, bless that person in return. When others mistreat and harass you, accept it as your mission to pray for them. To those who despise you, continue to serve them and minister to them.* (Luke 6:27-29 TPT)

I assume that if you are this far in the book, you have already chosen to spread more of Christ's love to your family and friends. Well done!

But here's a tough question: How many of you have tried these practices with your "enemies"? This mandate may be the most demanding of Jesus' commandments. *Do good to those who hate you.* Loving your enemies will take the practices in this book to a whole new level.

To get the full significance of Jesus' radical command, let's remember the context in which he pronounced it. Jesus lived under one of the cruelest, most tyrannical governments known to man. He would have grown up seeing people in his community whipped, beaten, stoned, imprisoned under inconceivable conditions and nailed to crosses. (And we worry about what *our* kids see these days!) The Jewish people endured a spirit-busting tax rate with none of the subsequent social services we receive from our government. Their harsh rulers generally didn't worship their God, but were polytheists who spent their tax dollars on lavish temples to useless idols. This was who Jesus' audience would have been visualizing when he commanded, "…love your enemies." Many of the people hoped Jesus would *rid them* of this enemy. This teaching must have been beyond their comprehension.

In continuing to fathom who we must love, a man asked Jesus, "*Who is my neighbor?*" as he finished telling his audience the command to "*love your neighbor.*" Jesus answered with a parable, an illustrative story, in which a *Samaritan* was the hero who best showed love (Remember the story of The Good Samaritan from Luke 10:30-37 that I paraphrased for you in the first chapter?). Interesting choice.

Samaritans were not merely outcasts; the Jews *despised* them.[xliii] They were of half Jewish/half Gentile ethnicity, and they worshipped pagan gods. When the Jews returned from their exile to Babylon and began to rebuild the temple, Samaritans poured pig's blood throughout the sacred temple area, defiling it and requiring the Jews to halt construction to consecrate it. Samaritans were **more reviled than the Romans**.

Jesus commanded us to love *everyone*, even our enemies and people who repulse us. In the 21st Century who are our "enemies"? Who are those who hate us? My personal list would include human traffickers, MS-13 gang members, doctors who perform abortions and members of the Chinese Communist Party. In our highly polarized, post-COVID-19 world you might add the neighbor who voted for "the other guy," or the person who refused to wear a mask.

Maybe your enemy is not someone out to kill you, but someone who is **threatening your core values**. How do you view those who want to destroy the family structure or your freedom of speech? How do you perceive LGBTQ individuals, or people who revile LGBTQ people? Do you consider members of Antifa or White Supremacists your enemies?

I've noticed a human tendency. I think we hate groups and then judge individuals based on what group we think—or assume—they belong to. We take in the visual data about a person, their outward appearance, then run up our Ladder of Inference (in Words and Impressions) assign him/her to a group and conclude: he is [a group label] so he is my "enemy" or he is my friend. It's much harder to hate an individual than a vague group.

What group of people do you find it challenging to love? If talking directly to you, who would Jesus have made the unlikely hero in Luke 10 to get your attention?

God is a Good Teacher

It is with profound embarrassment I confess to you I had strong negative biases about a specific group—our area's homeless population. I had adopted a belief that this group was comprised of drug addicts and alcoholics who just needed to get clean and get a job. I sought data to support that belief as I walked past people sitting on the sidewalk with cardboard signs. I was stuck in my Reflexive Loop, and I couldn't "see" any data that might contradict that belief. See the Ladder of Inference description on page 68, for a reminder on this unfortunate thinking pattern of biases and stereotypes.

I was on the board of an organization that was asked to help clean up the Boulder Creek corridor, a well-known camping area for the homeless people in town. I remember being singularly unenthusiastic about the assignment. The organization also wanted someone to photograph the Saturday project, so I quickly volunteered my husband, a professional photographer. I knew David would do an excellent job and it would reassure me to have him along on this unpleasant task. He had similar prejudices as I did but is philanthropic by nature and was curious.

When we arrived, the organizers gave me a trash bag along with latex gloves and told me to head east on Boulder Creek. They steered my husband in the opposite direction and asked him to take pictures of the project. I was on my own. As I approached the tent for volunteers, I was introduced to a homeless person who would work alongside me. That was a surprise! Here was an individual from the group I "hated," but he didn't seem to fit my stereotypical homeless person. He was willing to do some hard work. He was pleasant to talk to and didn't appear addicted.

What an eye-opening day! I met several of my co-worker's friends who were also homeless. They were interesting, friendly people. I listened to their descriptions of what caused them to be living on the street and recognized that they each had walked a different path.

On our short drive home, David and I were debriefing our day and commenting on the various circumstances that had caused our fellow laborers to lose their homes. Suddenly and emphatically, David declared, "We have to do a book. We have to photograph members of Boulder's homeless community and tell their stories. People need to know their *unique* stories."

Now to be clear, we had never written a book, never talked about writing a book, and didn't know the first thing about how to publish a book. But God had given David a vision for a project that he was determined to carry out. Yes, we brought a few relevant skills to such a project—Dave took portraits and covered weddings as a business, and I wrote training curriculum. But we were busy! We both had full-time leadership consulting jobs that had us traveling the country two-three weeks each month. I felt like Moses arguing with God in front of the burning bush about how ill-equipped we were. God was not deterred. And neither was my dear husband.

We spent 2011 fulfilling this vision and witnessing miracle after miracle. God had shifted our focus from a stereotyped group to individuals. We met people who worked in Boulder's non-profits who were committed to making life on the street survivable and who worked tirelessly to move folks into housing and jobs. They introduced us to over 60 homeless residents who volunteered to be photographed and tell us their stories. I created a team of local authors who helped me write the stories.

God brought us professionals who volunteered their services, including an editor, designer, and artist for our book cover. We self-published the book with funds we—well, God—raised. Our church hosted a book-signing party where those featured in the book signed their photographs for the people celebrating with us. It was a full and extraordinary year. All the proceeds of the 500 books we sold went to two Boulder charities that serve the homeless.

This humble project changed us forever. With God's nudge, we met *individuals* in a *group* we had previously labeled as worthless, alcoholic and drug addicted. We met a woman who had lost her daughter through an unsolved murder, a concert violinist from San Francisco, a mentally ill former Harvard professor, a young man "born to a 16-year-old woman and the man who left her when I was 3-days-old," and a musician who just liked the freedom of the "camping life". We met people who were obviously self-medicating, but we saw beneath the surface that their pain was the result of deep life wounds. Instead of making judgments about a faceless American sub-group, we now saw these people as valued individuals, uniquely created and loved by God. We titled our book, *Until They Have Faces: Stories of Recovery, Resilience and Redemption.*

The project changed the people in the book as well. Picture an unshaved, disheveled 50-something man under a bridge, surrounded by photography lights, and me fussing over him to strike a good pose. Then sitting down with me on his sleeping bag while he told me his story. Our participants had pride in being in a book and having folks in Boulder come up to them to sign their picture. **They felt more known and loved** than they may have ever felt in their lives. Several of them said they felt a stronger motivation to get off the street. A year later, the two charities asked us to do a second printing as a fund-raiser for them. Many of those who were still in the area asked us to include an addendum, noting how they had improved their lives.

Two verses come to mind:

> *The Lord does not look at the things people look at. People look at the outward appearance, but the Lord looks at the heart.* (1 Samuel 16:7 NIV)

> *Live in harmony with one another. Do not be proud, but* ***be willing to associate with people of low position.*** *Do not be conceited.... live at peace with everyone.* (Romans 12:16-18 NIV)

I learned a powerful lesson that year from my patient heavenly Father about looking at people's hearts rather than their outward appearances. I also learned about how to position myself in humility before God.

Choosing to Let God Judge

One of the most common objections I hear when I encourage others to befriend someone different from them, an "enemy" or someone they dislike, is that they fear it would condone their lifestyle. Let's think about that. Are you friends with someone who is divorced? Overeats? Over drinks? Lies a bit more than you prefer? Has had an affair? Is judgmental? Has cheated on her taxes? Overspends?

We are all sinners. Our *friends* are all sinners. Jesus' friends were sinners. We can love the sinner—be compassionate, kind and respectful—**without having to accept their beliefs or lifestyle choices as ours.** When I show Christ's love to my Muslim neighbor, my transgender co-worker, or my local abortionist, I am not denying God's Word. *I am doing what it says.* I am not condoning their lifestyle—or judging it—I am choosing to embrace Jesus's command to love one another.

Jesus was unambiguous:

> *Do not judge and criticize and condemn [others unfairly with an attitude of self-righteous superiority, as though assuming the office of a judge], so that you will not be judged [unfairly]. For just as you [hypocritically] judge others [when you are sinful and unrepentant], so will you be judged; and in accordance with your standard of measure [used to pass out judgment], judgment will be measured to you.* (Matthew 7:1-2 AMP)

Always Learning

I was making my way through an airport I had never been in, frantic that I would miss my connecting plane. The signage was poor, and the minutes were quickly ticking by. As I hurried along, I called my daughter who was meeting me on the other end for a much-anticipated girls' weekend. I told her how lost and panicky I was (She's a master at empathy!) My body language screamed, "I'm lost!" as I scanned the area for someone who might help me. I am sure I was unconsciously looking for people "like me."

Who came to my rescue? A black man with maroon-colored hair wearing a hot pink satin blouse, glittery blue bell-bottom pants, black platform boots and over-sized turquoise-sequined glasses. He had several large silver-beaded necklaces on his chest. "I couldn't help overhearing you," he said as he leaned toward me. "I used to work here, and it's a pretty confusing airport. Can I show you how to get to your gate?"

He walked me to the underground tram, ushered me outside on the tarmac, trudged with me down a quarter-mile terminal, and kindly deposited me right at my gate. I never would have found it on my own. Who am I to judge how angels look?

Being Judged

Has it occurred to you that others are judging *you*? How does your "enemy" judge you? Wouldn't it be wonderful if, as you walked away from a conversation with a stranger on the street, you heard him comment, "He was awfully nice for a Christian!"

As part of writing our book, we met the Executive Director of one of the many Boulder charities that serve the homeless. She educated us and bridged the gap between the people we wanted to interview, who tended to have low trust, and us. We spent many weekends wandering the streets of Boulder with her. I assumed she had a different worldview than me based on our conversations and her profession.

A few months into our relationship, she "friended" me on Facebook. I knew when I hit the "accept" button that she would see my profile that listed me as part of a group, a "conservative Christian," and that it would likely surprise her. I also knew she might make (false) assumptions about me based on that affiliation. I waited until we next saw each other in person.

"Samantha, I know I haven't gotten back to you about connecting on Facebook. I'm going to friend you, but I wanted to let you know I define myself as a conservative Christian in my profile."

"I thought you might be a Christian," she exclaimed, "But you're not a *conservative* Christian!"

She had a reflexive loop, a bias against conservative Christians that I had, through God's grace, shattered through my interactions with her. Her negative perception of conservative Christians (as a group) didn't match the person she had befriended. That's my idea of magnetic witnessing, and one of my life goals is to have more stories like this.

How Do We Show Love to Our Enemy?

As I've shared, a chief desire of humanity is to be known and loved. It's a longing planted in our hearts by God. Only he can perfectly fulfill that yearning completely, but he can use us to carry it out. Do you know what our homeless friends told us they most want from the people who pass them on the street? They want **eye contact and a smile;** to be seen; to experience the dignity given to every other pedestrian. That doesn't require time or money, just a *completely different attitude.*

> *And if you greet only your brothers [wishing them God's blessing and peace], what more [than others] are you doing? Do not even the Gentiles [who do not know the Lord] do that? You, therefore, will be perfect [growing into spiritual maturity both in mind and character, actively integrating godly values into your daily life], as your heavenly Father is perfect.* (Matthew 5:47-48 AMP)

Should you go out and introduce yourself to the gang member dealing drugs on the corner? No. But if you see someone at your local restaurant that *looks* like a gang member, or is wearing a T-shirt that disgusts you, **make eye contact and smile**. Or you might ask if you can sit with them and hear their story. Choose to make people feel known and appreciated.

More Lessons from God

As I made my way onto yet another airplane and toward my coveted aisle seat, I saw that my middle seat mate was a 20-something white male with red hair to his shoulders and quarter-sized gauges in his ears. A young black male was at the window seat. (Do you hear the data I've selected?)

As I buckled my seatbelt, the redhead reached over the seat to mess with the hair of the guy in front of him. *Ugh! What am I in for?* I thought. I couldn't tell you what another person on that plane looked like. It wasn't relevant to me. I selected the data that was important to me—the person with whom I would spend three hours. *I have nothing in common with these guys*, I thought. *It's going to be a long flight.* I got out my headphones and opened my book. Then the Holy Spirit convicted me. *Why don't you try a conversation?*

Where do I start? I wondered. I had been curious about gauges, so in the most non-judgmental tone of voice I could muster I asked, "I've been wondering about gauges. What made you want to have them?" (OK. Not the most eloquent start, I admit, but at least it was a start.) "My mother asked me the same thing!" he responded in a warm, friendly way. "I don't know why."

Good news, I thought. *He has a mother who cares about him. Where do I go from here, Lord?* My companion then dropped his seat tray down and slapped a book on it, *Jesus Among Other Gods* by Ravi Zacharias[1]. *Whoa! New data.* I had read Zacharias myself. He was a deep Christian thinker. But my young seatmate was probably just exploring all religions. Do you hear me making loads of assumptions? I checked in with the Spirit, garnered my courage and spoke. "Interesting book. Who do you think Jesus is?"

"He's my Lord and Savior." *Mind blown.* God sure has a sense of humor! This was a Christian brother! I had judged him by his outward appearance. Now I had a look at his heart. We talked the rest of the flight. I learned that he and his pals, four of them traveling together, were members of the Christian metal rock band, Kronicles. By

---

[1] *I am aware that since Zacharius's death in 2020, there have been disturbing allegations of grave sexual misconduct. He was a Christian apologist, author, and a sinner.*

the end of our flight, he asked to friend me on Facebook!

The best way to break our negative biases is to seek data (more information) that is contrary to what we expect. We have to choose to look for the opposite of what our biases are looking to confirm. That choice is an intentional act of love. Another way to think of it is to give others the benefit of the doubt. It requires us to spend more time with people very different from us.

When we lower our guard and let go of our biases, we learn other perspectives on the world and how they were formed. We'll better understand our "enemy's" life experiences, wounds, and subsequent Ladder of Inference. It will turn uninformed indifference or hate into appreciation and empathic love.

Will we agree with everything we hear? Probably not. Do we have to condone the life decisions the person has made? Absolutely not. It's their life and they are individually accountable to God, not to us. But we *will* come away with more compassion, more understanding, and we will have done what love requires. God looks at **individual hearts**. Let's choose to do that, too.

Social Media: Where Hate Lives

What we wouldn't choose to say to a friend over lunch or a stranger on a plane—we *will* say to our "friends" on social media. What's that about? Remember our communication formula? When we communicate on social media, the only thing our audience can "hear" are our words which make up only 7% of our message. We lose body language and tone of voice. A full 93% of the message is missing. What may sound funny in our heads when said with clever sarcasm in our tone, can be perceived very differently when received through the limited written word.

Social media is also a one-sided conversation. We can't see our audience, which makes for a flawed mental filter as we write. We do not see our 'listeners' body language when we dump our opinions in their laps. We let loose our words without considering how they are "hitting" each of our 200-10,000 "friends." We say more than we would, more strongly than we should, without the benefit of our grandmother's horrified facial expression, or the deflated, hurt look in the eyes of our high school friend we haven't spoken to in years.

When we have a two-way, in-person conversation and can see how our words impact the other person, we choose to adjust our words, tone of voice and body language. We constantly adjust to warm our listener to our point of view.

Similarly, when we are the reader/listener on social media, we may see a post that is a body blow to our core values and our emotions skyrocket. We are compelled to get the "truth" out (at least I do) and respond before pausing. This is a splendid example of the ping pong game of your opinion, my opinion, your opinion with MORE CAPITALS, and my opinion with more exclamation marks!!!! Nothing about this exchange is loving.

Even when you choose to use the Word of God in your response, without the benefit of your tone of voice, Bible verses can leave your reader with an unintended negative impression. You can come across as a righteous Pharisee or be written off as a nut case. Trust me, I've tried it.

Choosing Love on Social Media

Posting on social media demands we don our Respond-ability Superpower cape and pause for an hour—or a day—to listen for the Spirit's answer to, "What does love require of me?" We make an enormous impact for Christ by intentionally seeking to respond with grace rather than hatred.

The best choice is to get off these platforms—the movie *The Social Dilemma* makes a compelling case for this. Let's start talking to real friends by phone or in person. The COVID shutdowns resulted in an even greater addiction to Facebook, Instagram, Snapchat and the like, but they are as unhealthy as licking a bannister. Hearing people's voices and seeing responses on their faces is exceedingly better for your mental, emotional and spiritual health!

Choosing to neither post nor respond is the wisest choice on social media. In the chapter More EQ, Please, we learned emotions rise when core values are involved. We can get a visceral reaction from reading a post, or, conversely, create a strong emotional reaction in others when we post. Relationships are broken. Remember, it's critical to at least add the phone as a communication mode to add tone of voice to an emotional interchange. The phone also makes it a two-way conversation and you can hear how your words affect the other person in real time. That feedback is invaluable in demonstrating love.

My Experience

Recently, I was having a "debate" on email with a close friend. I stayed calm and rational and used questions to seek to understand. As our email conversation continued, I could "hear" my friend getting more and more incensed. I *finally* remembered to pick up the phone. After a useful and meaningful 45-minute conversation she asked, "Can we keep talking about these issues [through email]?" I hesitated—an unconscious but valuable pause. Then she added, "Well, maybe we should speak by phone so we can hear each other's hearts." Perfect!!

God commands us to love people who are different from us—even those who hate us. Showing love where there is yet to be a relationship is as simple as a warm smile, honest eye contact and a "hello." It doesn't take time or money, just a renewed mind and an attitude attuned to the Holy Spirit.

By the way, remember how Jesus ended his lesson of the Good Samaritan:

> "*Which of these three* [who came upon the beaten man] *do you think proved himself a neighbor to the man who encountered the robbers?" He* [the attorney who had

made the initial inquiry] *answered, "The one who showed compassion and mercy to him." Then Jesus said to him,* ***"Go and constantly do the same."*** (Luke 10:37 AMP)

Self-reflection

1. What are you taking away from this chapter? Ask the Holy Spirit where he wants you to grow.

2. What group of people do you find challenging to love?

3. I find reading fiction gives me greater empathy and understanding about people who differ from me. Catherine Ryan Hyde, Charles Martin and Jodi Picoult are authors who come to mind. What books have you read that have helped you gain compassion and empathy for those different from you?

Exercise

Take a field trip to your local city. As you walk the streets, make eye contact and smile at people you would normally avoid. What happened? How did it affect your heart?

CHAPTER FIFTEEN

TYING IT ALL TOGETHER

> *I am giving you a new commandment, that you love one another. Just as I have loved you, so you too are to love one another. By this everyone will know that you are My disciples, if you have love and unselfish concern for one another.* (John 13:34-35 AMP)

When I read these words from Jesus, I long to have been one of his disciples with their first-hand look at perfect love in action. Sometimes, if I try hard, I can envision Jesus as he leans in to listen well; I can hear him ask meaningful questions as he sits around the evening fire sharing laughter and life with his band of twelve.

Imagine being captivated when hearing him calmly, and thoughtfully share ideas, answers, and even reproof—through stories, rather than long pompous diatribes. I ponder how it would be on the receiving end of his emotional maturity, as he offered authentic, flawless empathy to those who felt marginalized and forgotten… and I envision him generously offering that to me.

Truly Jesus was the Son of God, not arguing as they hauled him in front of the Sanhedrin, not cursing as they nailed his hands and feet to a wooden cross. It was from that cross that he said, *Father, forgive them.* I yearn to witness with my own eyes this costly forgiveness—not only for his friends as they tripped and stumbled over his determined path to the cross, but also for his murderous enemies.

I consider what it might have been like when, after seeing even the wickedest people and the worst behaviors, Jesus would pause, turn his heart and mind to his Father, and then respond in pure love. If I had seen Jesus loving his enemies, would I get it? Would it come easier for me? I have read in God's Word how he processed emotions with his Father and grieved even to the point of sweating blood—so I know he did. And finally, I ache for the privilege of quietly watching him in many private moments when he acknowledged the lowly and the insecure, showing them, "You are known and loved."

My friend, the world needs love. It always has. It always will. Jesus came to show us how to spread it lavishly so that his followers might represent him well. I pray that because of reading this book you choose to reflect Jesus' love to a greater extent and make love an action verb so that the people God puts in your life will truly feel known and loved.

> *My dear children, let's not just talk about love; let's practice real love. This is the only way we'll know we're living, truly living in God's reality.* (I John 3:18 MSG)

Our Practical Tools to Follow God's Path

Before responding to a stimulus, pause to check in with the Holy Spirit. Ask, "What does love require of me?" (Chapters 1 & 7)

> *But the Helper (Comforter, Advocate, Intercessor—Counselor, Strengthener, Standby), the Holy Spirit, whom the Father will send in My name [in My place, to represent Me and act on My behalf], He will teach you all things. And He will help you remember everything that I have told you.* (John 14:26 AMP)

Use other-focused listening often. When emotions are involved, use hyper-focused listening. (Chapter 2)

> *Post this at all the intersections, dear friends: Lead with your ears, follow up with your tongue, and let anger straggle along*

> *in the rear.* (James 1:19 MSG)

Be curious about others. Ask non-judgmental questions beginning with What and How. (Chapter 3)

Remember that when you speak, you are giving *your perspective.* Use, "What am I missing?" to acknowledge this and seek the other person's perspective.

Be mindful of your body language and dress. Say, "I love you," without saying a word. (Chapter 4)

> *Be devoted to one another in love. Honor one another above yourselves.* (Romans 12:10 NIV)

Sincerely acknowledge at least one person each day. Be a role model of common courtesy (Chapter 5)

> *Sitting down, Jesus called the Twelve and said, "Anyone who wants to be first must be the very last, and the servant of all."* (Mark 9:35 NIV)

In every conversation, with others and with God, balance your listening, asking and speaking. (Chapter 6)

Understand this, my beloved brothers and sisters. Let everyone be quick to hear [be a careful, thoughtful listener], slow to speak [a speaker of carefully chosen words and], slow to anger [patient, reflective, forgiving]. (James 1:19 AMP)

Use your powers of observation about your emotions and other's emotions to inform how to respond in love. (Chapter 7)

Use your core values to understand your own emotional reactions and how to be more content. Learn the core values of others and honor them as much as possible. (Chapter 8)

Here is a simple, rule-of-thumb guide for behavior: Ask yourself what you want people to do for you, then grab the initiative and do it for ***them****.* (Matthew 7:12a MSG)

Be generous with your attitude. Create margin in your life to be available for divine appointments. (Chapter 9)

Do everything readily and cheerfully—no bickering, no second-guessing allowed! Go out into the world uncorrupted, a breath of fresh air in this squalid and polluted society.

Provide people with a glimpse of good living and of the living God. Carry the light-giving Message into the night so I'll have good cause to be proud of you on the day that Christ returns. (Philippians 2:14-16 MSG)

Recognize and name a person's feelings before pointing out facts or offering solutions. (Chapter 10)

Therefore, as God's chosen people, holy and dearly loved, clothe yourselves with compassion, kindness, humility, gentleness and patience. (Colossians 3:10 NIV)

Be thoughtful in conflict. Gain clarity on your own and other's perspectives. Share your perspective and ask, "How did you see it?" (Chapter 11)

Offer your bodies as a living sacrifice, holy and pleasing to God, this is your true and proper worship. Do not conform to the pattern of this world, but be transformed by the renewing of your mind… Be devoted to one another in love. Honor one another above yourselves. (Romans 12:1-2, 10 NIV)

Be direct and kind with feedback, giving the gift of information. (Chapter 12)

You, my brothers and sisters, were called to be free. But do not use your freedom to indulge the flesh; rather, ***serve one another humbly in love****.* (Galatians 5:13 NIV)

Lament and forgive. Have a conversation with God and give him the authority to punish. Ask forgiveness with humility. (Chapter 13)

> *Get rid of all bitterness, rage and anger, brawling and slander, along with every form of malice. Be kind and compassionate to one another, forgiving each other, just as in Christ God forgave you.* (Ephesians 4:31-32 NIV)

When you catch yourself judging someone, thank the Holy Spirit for helping you realize it, then smile and make eye contact, and/or start a conversation. (Chapter 14)

> *Do not judge and criticize and condemn [others unfairly with an attitude of self-righteous superiority as though assuming the office of a judge], so that you will not be judged [unfairly].* (Matthew 7:1 AMP)

* * *

Jesus wants our faith to be active in the world, life affirming, and a light on the hill. You can do this! He left us with a Counselor so that in every interaction, before every statement or response, we can choose to pause and ask the Holy Spirit: "What does love require of me?"

This generation is famished for love—love in action. As

Christ-followers, let us be known as people who choose to display love with lavish abandon everywhere we go!

NEXT STEPS

I am excited to hear your stories about how the Holy Spirit directs you in using the tools presented here, or ideas you have for more ways to choose love. Please send them to me at my email address below and let me know if I may share them.

If you'd like the direct links to the books I've recommended, see my website Elle-Page.com.

Elle@Elle-Page.com

APPENDIX A

Optional Ways to Read This Book

Through this book I have examined foundational skills and tools to show love. There are reflection questions throughout and exercises for you to build and strengthen your love muscles. As you reflect with the Holy Spirit on how you best learn, choose one of these approaches to reading this book—or make up one that works best for you!

1. Read it straight through without doing the Reflections or Exercises—This will give you an overview and a fresh way of evaluating your daily interactions with God's people.

2. Read it a bit more thoughtfully and slowly, doing the Reflections and Exercises—This will help you build and strengthen your love muscles. You will more readily recognize those opportunities to pause and choose how you will demonstrate love.

3. Read through the Chapter titles and with the help of the Spirit choose a few areas in which you'd like to grow.
    - The topics that are most challenging to you. This might provide more focused attention to places you could grow the most.
    - The topics that you already do well or naturally. Neuroscientists tell us we gain the most learning when we focus on what we already do well.
    - Start with tools that you admire in others; that make you feel loved and you want to do as well as you've experienced.
4. Read it as in #2, above, and then teach the concepts and tools to your friend(s) or children to anchor the learning for yourself.
5. Read it as a Book Club or Bible Study and use the Self-reflection questions for your discussions.

APPENDIX B

Emotion Words

PLEASANT EMOTIONS

OPEN	HAPPY	ALIVE	GOOD
Understanding	Great	Playful	Calm
Confident	Joyous	Courageous	Peaceful
Reliable	Lucky	Energetic	Comfortable
Easy	Fortunate	Liberated	Pleased
Amazed	Delighted	Optimistic	Encouraged
Free	Overjoyed	Provocative	Reassured
Sympathetic	Cheerful	Impulsive	Surprised
Interested	Thankful	Free	Content
Satisfied	Important	Animated	Quiet
Receptive	Ecstatic	Spirited	Certain
Kind	Jubilant	Thrilled	Relaxed
Comforted	Festive	Blessed	Serene

LOVE	**INTEREST-ED**	**POSITIVE**	**STRONG**
Loving	Concerned	Eager	Free
Considerate	Fascinated	Excited	Sure
Affectionate	Intrigued	Earnest	Certain
Sensitive	Absorbed	Intent	Rebellious
Tender	Inquisitive	Anxious	Unique
Devoted	Nosy	Inspired	Dynamic
Attracted	Engrossed	Determined	Tenacious
Passionate	Curious	Enthusiastic	Hardy
Admiration	Challenged	Brave	Secure
Warm	Sympathy	Daring	Bold
Touched	Comforted	Hopeful	
		Optimistic	

DIFFICULT/UNPLEASANT EMOTIONS

ANGRY	**DEPRESSED**	**CONFUSED**	**HELPLESS**
Irritated	Lousy	Upset	Incapable
Enraged	Disappointed	Doubtful	Alone
Hostile	Discouraged	Uncertain	Paralyzed
Fuming	Ashamed	Indecisive	Fatigued
Indignant	Powerless	Perplexed	Useless
Annoyed	Diminished	Embarrassed	Inferior
Upset	Guilty	Hesitant	Vulnerable
Hateful	Dissatisfied	Shy	Empty
Unpleasant	Miserable	Disillusioned	Dominated
Offensive	Detestable	Unbelieving	Distressed
Bitter	Repugnant	Skeptical	Forced
Aggressive	Despicable	Distrustful	Woeful
Resentful	Disgusting	Lost	Pathetic
Inflamed	Terrible	Unsure	Tragic
Provoked	Sulky	Uneasy	Tense
Infuriated	Bad	Pessimistic	

INDIFFER -ENT	**AFRAID**	**HURT**	**SAD**
Insensitive	Fearful	Crushed	Tearful
Dull	Terrified	Tormented	Sorrowful
Nonchalant	Suspicious	Deprived	Pained
Neutral	Anxious	Pained	Grief
Reserved	Alarmed	Rejected	Anguish
Weary	Panic	Offended	Desperate
Bored	Nervous	Victimized	Unhappy
Preoccupied	Worried	Humiliated	Lonely
Cold	Frightened	Alienated	Mournful
Disinterested	Threatened	Injured	Dismayed
Lifeless	Cowardly	Aching	Heartbroken
Dejected	Shaky		Wronged

ACKNOWLEDGEMENTS

I want to express my deepest gratitude to:

My writing team

- Jodi Burnett, author and mentor, for your early encouragement and sage advice. Visit **www.Jodi-Burnett.com** to see her "suspense with a spark of romance" books.
- Pam Cray, editor and pastor, for your expert eye on the whole, and astute suggestions.
- David Page, my husband, for your wisdom, support, patience and thoughtful feedback.
- Kendall Pischke, daughter and Cheerleader-in-Chief, for always being there when I needed a jolt of encouragement or perseverance.
- Cindy Probasco, editor, and friend, for your comprehensive, meticulous, and insightful recommendations.

My supportive, discerning Beta Readers who provided perceptive comments and final proofing:

Laura Barnes
Tina Beard
Stephanie Gregg
Carla Hopkins
Laura Jesberg
Dan Schmidt
Julie Sodestrom

My family and friends who endured endlesss conversations about content, concepts and stories. Thank you for your support, interest, patience and love.

ABOUT THE AUTHOR

Elle Page is a consultant, speaker, trainer, author, and executive coach committed to creating healthy relationships, teams, and organizations. For 20 years she was a Senior Consultant and Executive Coach with CI International and is currently Vice President of Engage Leadership, Inc. She worked on the staff of the Secretary of Education in the Reagan Administration, and for a Congresswoman in her district office. Her volunteer activities include coaching pastors and mentoring young moms through MOPS International. Elle has been a follower of Jesus since high school. She married her college sweetheart, and they have two married children and six grandchildren. Elle has lived on both coasts but has made Colorado her home for the past 28 years. Elle is a pickleball addict, a voracious reader, an archer, hiker, and kayaker.

If you would like Elle to attend your book club virtually or speak at your church or conference, contact her through her website Elle-Page.com

ENDNOTES

Chapter 1

[i] Andy Stanley, North Point Community Church (Alpharetta, GA)

[ii] Ibid.

[iii] Sarah Young, *Jesus Calling* (Thomas Nelson, 2004), 35.

Chapter 2

[iv] Jennifer Romig, "*Listen Like a Lawyer, Speed of Speech<Speed of Thought*" (Sept 24, 2015), https://listenlikealawyer.com/2015/09/24/speed-of-speech-speed-of-thought/

[v] Young.

[vi] Frankl.

Chapter 3

[vii] Stephen R. Covey, *Seven Habits of Highly Effective People: Powerful Lessons in Personal Change* (2013)

Chapter 4

[viii] Albert Mehrabian; Morton Katz Wiener, Daniel (editor), "*Decoding of Inconsistent Communications,*" Journal of Personality and Social Psychology (1967) 6(1): 109-114.
Albert Mehrabian and Susan R. Ferris, *Inference of Attitudes from Nonverbal Communication in Two Channels,* Journal of Consulting Psychology (1967) 31(3): 249-252.

[ix] John T. Molloy, *Dress for Success* (P. H. Wyden, 1975).

[x] Carol Kinsey Goman, *Seven Seconds to Make a First Impression, Forbes Magazine*, Feb. 13, 2011, https://www.forbes.com/sites/carolkinseygoman/2011/02/13/seven-seconds-to-make-a-first-impression/?sh=77c333a72722

[xi] Mehrabian.

[xii] Chris Argyris, quoted by Peter M. Senge, *The Fifth Discipline: The Art & Practice of The Learning Organization* (Doubleday, 2006) 242-246.
https://synergycommons.net/resources/the-ladder-of-inference/

Chapter 5

[xiii] *Exploring Your Mind, Sawubona: An African Tribe's Beautiful Greeting*, 17 October 2018 https://exploringyourmind.com/sawubona-african-tribe-greeting/

[xiv] Wikipedia, https://en.wikipedia.org/wiki/Ostracism#Modern_usage

Chapter 6

[xv] Ibid, 385-391.

[xvi] The Myers & Briggs Foundation, https://www.myersbriggs.org/my-mbti-personality-type/mbti-basics/

[xvii] Ibid.

[xviii] Mehrabian.

[xix] https://www.prayerandpossibilities.com/lectio-divina-prayer/

Chapter 7

[xx] Daniel Goleman, *Emotional Intelligence: Why It Can Matter More Than IQ* (Bantam, 2005)
[xxi] Viktor Frankl.

[xxii] Brené Brown, *Daring Greatly: How the Courage to Be Vulnerable Transforms the Way We Live, Love, Parent, and Lead* (Avery, 2015)

Chapter 8

[xxiii] Brené Brown, https://www.ted.com/talks/brené_brown_the_power_of_vulnerability.

[xxiv] Ibid.

[xxv] Effectiviology, https://effectiviology.com/fundamental-attribution-error/

Chapter 9

[xxvi] The Peak Performance Center https://thepeakperformancecenter.com/educational-learning/learning/process/stages/

[xxvii] Richard Swenson, M.D., *Margin: Restoring Emotional, Physical, Financial, and Time Reserves to Overloaded Lives* (NavPress, 2004)

[xxviii] Theresa Wiseman, "Jan: Leading Global Nursing Research, A Concept Analysis of Empathy," (1996)

Chapter 10

[xxix] Terry Wardle, Ph.D., ***Wounded: How to Find Wholeness and Inner Healing in Christ*** (Leafwood, 2005)
[xxx] Ibid.

[xxxi] John Burke, *Imagine Heaven: Near-Death Experiences, God's Promises, and the Exhilarating Future That Awaits You* (Baker Books, 2015).

[xxxii] Kim Scott, *Radical Candor* (St. Martin's Press, 2019)

Chapter 12

[xxxiii] Bryant H. McGill, *Simple Reminders: Inspiration for Living Your Best Life* (2018)

Chapter 13

[xxxiv] Dr. David Stoop, *Forgiving What You'll NEVER Forget* (Revell, 2017) 44-45.

[xxxv] Ibid.

[xxxvi] Ibid, 26-29.

[xxxvii] Ibid, 36-38.

[xxxviii] Ibid, 39-41.

[xxxix] Ibid, 43-59.

[xl] Dr. William James, philosopher and psychologist, (January 11, 1842–August 26, 1910) **https://www.goodreads.com/quotes/108925-actions-seems-to-follow-feeling-but-really-actions-and-feeling**

[xli] Stoop. 18

[xlii] Carlos Whittaker, *Enter Wild*, Part II: Enter War (Waterbrook/Random House, 2020) 63-134.

Chapter 14

[xliii] Bible Study Tools, **https://www.biblestudytools.com/bible-study/topical-studies/the-samaritans-hope-from-the-history-of-a-hated-people.html**

Made in the USA
Middletown, DE
27 May 2023

31169661R00166